FAMILY ENVIRONMENT AND SCHOOL PERFORMANCE

FAMILY ENVIRONMENT AND SCHOOL PERFORMANCE

Taruna Choudhary Dhall

KALPAZ PUBLICATIONS
Delhi-110052

Family Environment and School Performance

Rs. 490

ISBN: 81-7835-256-7

Published in 2004 in India by
Kalpaz Publications,
C-30, Satyawati Nagar, Delhi-110052
E-mail : Kalpaz@hotmail.com

Laser Typesetting at : Shree Vaishnavi Creations, Delhi
Printed at : Mehra Offset Press, Delhi

Contents

List of Tables 7

Preface 13

1. **Introduction** **17**

Introuduction; Family environment; Family Environment and School Performance; Justification of the study; Statement of the Problem; Operational Definitions; Objectives of the Study; Hypotheses of the Study; Delimitation of the Study.

2. **Review of Related Litrature** **27**

3. **Plan and Procedure** **39**

Introduction; Methodology; Sampling; Tools used; Construction of Family Environment Scale; Family Environment Scale for Children; Family Environment Scale for Parents; Non Verbal Test of Intelligence; Socio Economic Status Inventory; Data Collection; Statistical Techniques used.

4. **Analysis, Interpretation and Discussion of Results** **49**

Introduction; School Performance of Elementary School Children Relation to their Family Environment, Intelligence and Socio-Economic Status; School Performance of Elementary School Children in Relation to Children's Perception of Family Environment; School Performance of Elementary School Children in Relation to Parents' Perception of Family Environment; School Performance of Elementary School Children in Relation to their Intelligence; Impact of Family Environment on School Performance of Elementary School Children; School Performance Differentials in Elementary School Children at Different Level of Family Environment (as Perceived by Children); School Performance Differentials of Elementary School Children at Different Levels of Family Environment as Perceived by Parents; Impact of Family Environment on the School Performance of Elementary School Children belonging to Similar Intelligence Group; School performance Differentials in Elementary School Children belonging to Similar intelligence group at different levels of Overall Family Environment (as perceived by children); School Performance Differentials in Elementary School Children belonging to Similar Intelligence Group at Different Levels of Five Dimensions of Family Environment (as perceived by Children); School Performance Differentials in Elementary School Children belonging to Similar Intelligence Group at Different Levels of Overall Family Environment (as perceived by Parents); School Performance Differentials in Elementary School Children belonging to Similar Intelligence Group at Different Levels of Five Dimensions of Family Environment as Perceived by Parents; Discussion of Results.

5. **Main Findings Educational Implications and Suggestion for Further Research** **129**

Main Findings; School Performance of Elementary School Children in Relation to their Family Environment, Intelligence and Socio-Economic Status; Impact of Family Environment on School Performance of Elementary School Children as Brought out by School Performance Differentials at Different Levels of Family Environment; Impact of Family Environment on School Performance of Elementary School Children Belonging to Similar Intelligence Groups as Brought out by School Performance Differentials at Different Levels of Family Environment (As Perceived by Children and Parents); Educational Implication; Suggestion for Further Research.

Summery 135

Introduction; Justification of the Study; Statement of the Problem; Operational Definition of the Terms Used; Family Environment; Objectives of the Study; Hypotheses; Delimitation of the Study; Method; Sample; Tools Used; Statistical Techniques Used; Main Findings; Educational Implication; Suggestion for Further Research.

Appendices 147

Bibliography 155

Index 165

List of Tables

3.1. Distribution of Items on Various Dimensions of First Draft of Family Environment Scale (Fes) For Children. 43

3.2. Distribution of Items on Various Dimensions of Final form of Family Environment Scale for Children. 44

4.1. Coefficients of Correlation Between School Performance of Elementary School Children and their Overall Family Environment and its Five Dimensions (As Perceived by Children) N = 185. 50

4.2. Coefficients of Correlation Between School Performance Elementary School Children and their Overall Family Environment and its Five Dimensions (As Perceived by Parents) N = 175. 52

4.3. Coefficients of Correlation Between School Performance of Elementary School Children and their Intelligence, N=185. 53

4.4. Coefficients of Correlation Between School Performance of Elementary School Children and their Socio-Economic Status, N=185. 53

4.5. Classification of Subjects into Three Groups in Terms of Their Score Value on Overall Family Environment and Its Five Dimension (as perceived by children) N = 185. 54

4.6. Classification of Subjects into Three Groups in Terms of Their Score Value on Overall Family Environment and Its Five Dimension (as perceived by parents) N = 175. 55

4.7. Significance of Difference in the Mean School Performance Scores of Elementary School Children at Different Level of (As Perceived by Children). 56

4.8. Significance of Difference in Mean School Performance Scores of Elementary School Children at Different Level of Family Environment on (As Perceived by Children). 57

4.9. Significance of Difference in Mean School Performance Scores of Elementary Schoool Children at Different Level of Family Environment on (As Perceived by Children). 59

4.10. Significance of Difference in Mean School Performance Scores of Elementary School Children at Different Level of Family Environment on (As Perceived by Children). 61

4.11. Significance of Difference in Mean School Performance Scores of Elementary School Children at Different Level of Family Environment on (As Perceived by Children). 63

4.12. Significance of Difference in Mean School Performance of Elementary School Children at Different Level of familyEnvironment on (As Perceived by Children). 64

4.13. Comparison of 't' Ratios Obtained for School Performance Different Level of their Family Environment with Respect to Overall Family Environment and its Five Dimension (As Perceived by Children). 66

4.14. Comparison of Mean School Performance Scores of Elementary SchoolChildren at Different Level of their Family Environment (As Perceived by Children). 66

4.15. Significance of Difference in Mean School Performance Scores of Elementary School Children at Different Levels of Overall Family Environment (As Perceived by Parents). 67

4.16. Significance of Difference in Mean School Performance Scores of Elementary School Children at Different Level of Family Environment on (As Perceived by Parents). 69

4.17. Significance of Difference in Mean School Performance Scores of Elementary School Children at Different Levels of Family Environment on (As Perceived by Parents). 71

4.18. Significance of Difference in Mean School Performance Scores of Elementary School Children at Different Levels of Family Environment on (As Perceived by Parents). 72

4.19. Significance of Difference in Mean School Performance Scores of Elementary School Children at Different Level of Family Environment on (As Perceived by Parents). 74

4.20. Significance of Difference in Mean School Performance Scores of Elementary School Children at Different Level of Family Environment on (As Perceived by Parents). 75

4.21. Comparison of 't' Ratios Obtained for School Performance Differentials of Elementary School Children at Different Level of their Family Environment with Respect to Overall Family

Environment and its Five Dimension (As Perceived by Parents). 76

4.22. Comparison of Mean School Performance Scores of Elementary School Children at Different Level of their Family Environment (As Perceived by Parents). 77

4.23. Classification of Subjects into Three Groups in Terms of their Intelligence Scores. 78

4.24. Significance of Difference in Mean School Performance Scores of Elementary School Children Belonging to High Intelligence Group at Different Levels of (As Perceived by Children). 79

4.25. Significance of Difference in Mean School Performance Scores of Elementary School Children Belonging to Moderate Intelligence Group at Different Levels of (As Perceived by Children). 80

4.26. Significance of Difference in Mean School Performance Scores of Elementary School Children Belonging to Low Intellegence at Different Level of (As Perceived by Children). 82

4.27. Comparisons of 't' Ratios, Obtained for School Performance Differential of Elementary School Children Belonging to Similar Intelligence Groups i.e., High; Moderate and Low, at Different Levels of their Family Environment (As Perceived by Children). 83

4.28. Comparison of Mean School Performance Scores of Elementary School Children Belonging to Similar Intelligence Group i.e. High, Moderate and Low and Experiencing Different Family Environment viz. Enriched, Moderate and Low (As Perceived by Children). 84

4.29. Significance of Difference in Mean School Performance Scores of Elementary School Children Belonging to High Intelligence Group at different Levels of Five Dimensions of Family Environment viz. Achievement Orientation; Cognitive Stimulation; Recreational Orientation; Home Structure; and Language Stimulation (As perceived by Children). 86

4.30. Significance of Difference in Mean School Performance Scores of Elementary School Children Belonging to Moderate Intelligence Group at Different Levels of Five Dimensions of Family Environment viz. Achievement Orientation; Cognitive Stimulation; Recreational Orientation; Home Structure; and

Language Stimulation (As perceived by Children). 91

4.31. Significance of Difference in Mean School Performance Scores of Elementary School Children Belonging to Low Intelligence Group at Different Levels of Five Dimensions of Family Environment viz. Achievement Orientation; Cognitive Stimulation; Recreational Orientation; Home Structure; and Language Stimulation (As perceived by Children). 95

4.32. Comparisons of 't' Ratios Obtained for School Performance Differentials of Elementary School Children Belonging to Similar Intelligence Group viz. High, Moderate and Low, at Different Levels of Family Environment i.e., Enriched, Moderate and Low with Respect to all the Five Dimension of Family Environment. (As Perceived by Children). 101

4.33. Comparison of Mean School Performance Scores of Elementary School Children Belonging to Similar Intelligence Group viz. High, Moderate and Low, and Experiencing Different Family Environment i.e., Enriched, Moderate and Low with Respect to Five Dimension of Family Environment (As Perceived by Children). 102

4.34. Significance of Difference in Mean School Performance Scores of Elementary School Children Belonging to High Intelligence Group at Different Levels of (As Perceived by Parents). 104

4.35. Significance of Difference in Mean School Performance Scores of Elementary School Children with Similar Intelligence Moderate Intelligence at Different Levels of (As Perceived by Parents). 105

4.36. Significance of Difference in Mean School Performance Scores of Elementary School Children with Similar Intelligence Low Intelligence at Different Level of (As Perceived by Parents). 107

4.37. Comparisons of 't' Ratio, Obtained for School Performance Differentials of Elementary School Children Belonging to Similar Intelligence Groups i.e., High; Moderate and Low Intelligence, at Different Level of Family Environment, with Respect to Overall Family Environment (As Perceived by Parents). 109

4.38. Comparison of Mean School Performance Scores of Elementary School Children Belonging to Similar Intelligence

Group i.e., High, Moderate and Low and Experiencing Different Family Environment viz. Enriched, Moderate and Low. (As Perceived by Parents). 109

4.39. Significance of Difference in Mean School Performance Scores of Elementary School Children Belonging to High Intelligence Group at Different Levels of Five Dimensions of Family Environment viz. Achievement Orientation; Cognitive Stimulation; Recreational Orientation; Home Structure; and Language Stimulation (As Perceived by Parents). 111

4.40. Significance of Difference in Mean School Performance Scores of Elementary School Children Belonging to Moderate Intelligence Group at Different Levels of Five Dimensions of Family Environment viz. Achievement Orientation; Cognitive Stimulation; Recreational Orientation; Home Structure; and Language Stimulation (As Perceived by Parents). 114

4.41. Significance of Difference in Mean School Performance Scores of Elementary School Children Belonging to Low Intelligence Group at Different Levels of Five Dimensions of Family Environment viz. Achievement Orientation; Cognitive Stimulation; Recreational Orientation; Home Structure; and Language Stimulation (As Perceived by Parents). 118

4.42. Comparisons of 't' Ratios Obtained for School Performance Differentials of Elementary School Children Belonging to Similar Intelligence Groups viz. High, Moderate and Low, at Different Levels of Family Environment i.e., Enriched, Moderate and Low with Respect to all the Five Dimension of Family Environment. (as percent by parents). 122

4.43. Comparison of Mean School Performance Scores of Elementary School Children Belonging to Similar Intelligence Group viz. High, Moderate and Low, and Experiencing Different Family Environment i.e., Enriched, Moderate and Low with Respect to Five Dimension of Family Environment (as perceived by parents). 123

Preface

Education primarily is a process that is aimed at the all round development of the child-mental, physical and emotional. The individual child is after all what the whole process of education is centered around. A universal explanation forwarded by various educational thinkers concerning the process of education is that it is an important social activity planned and shared by parents, teachers, School committee and member of the community. Educational growth of the child and factors that influence its course are concerns that have long occupied the minds of people concerned with the process of education. Accordingly increasing concern hAs been expressed about the effectiveness and efficiency of teaching-learning outcomes of a system of education, which can be assessed in Terms of student's School Performance.

One of the most common beliefs is that the development of the child As considered from the point of view of competitive societies depends on what goes on in a School in Terms of the curriculum transacted; through teaching-learning, other activities, student-teacher interactions etc. That is why, perhaps, most parents seek and want their Children to be sent for better Schooling, particularly to Schools with the best available infrastructure and teachers. It is common knowledge that even in the same or Similar School environments the School Performance of Children varies considerably. A perception like this is indicative enough of the fact that School Performance of the child is influenced by a number of factors, some of which are personal to the individual while many others lie in the Environmentin which the learning take place. Such a situation calls for a search for factors other than School that create a Differenceor are associated with the Performance of Children at School. One naturally looks for the environments of vital Significance.

The Family of the child is a continuous and universal social setting influencing the learning process of the child directly or indirectly. Family not only provides for the primary needs of the individual but is also an institution that looks after the child's socialization and initial education.

It is here that his basic ideAs and ideals are initiated. As well As the many attitudes towards himself and his associates that determine his later adjustment to School and other out-of-home situations. In other words it can be said that one of the important aspects of learning process is the influence of Family upon the child's ability to learn.

Family EnvironmenthAs often been conceptualized As status variables, such As socio-Economic status. Broad static measures of socio-Economic status typically are used without a detailed examination of the behaviours and experiences that may differ or remain constant across socio-Economic Levels.

Societal changes brought about As a result of advancement in various aspects of the world around us have had a dramatic impact on Family Environmentin both developing and developed counties. This in turn hAs brought about a radical change in roles of Different Family member and parent-child interactions.

Families vary greatly in Structure and functioning. Variations exist also in School and in Children themselves. Therefore considering the complexity of the interaction between parent and child, and other factors, that might affect the development in the child in Terms of School Performance, many investigators have been inspired to explore further and identify dynamic ongoing processes within the larger network of Family interaction.

Research evidence concerning the role of various process variables points towards a direction where it can be argued with conviction that support for School Performance is possible in a range of families since parents contribute in Different ways to their child's Performance As it is not so much what parents use in Terms of socio-Economic status than what they actually do. The present investigation is an attempt to look into such related issues in the Indian context. Out of a variety of parent - child interactions only School focused parent-child interactions are proposed to be studied through Five Dimensions viz. Achievement Orientation, Cognitive Stimulation, Recreational Orientation, Home Structure and Language Stimulation.

Report of the study hAs been presented in five chapters. The first introductory chapter deals with the concept of Family Environment, relationship of Family Environment with School Performance, Objectives of the study, hypothesi formed and delimitation of the study. Second chapter deals with the review of related literature to find out the relevant issues to be probed into. Third chapter, Plan and Procedure, includes the methodology adopted for the study, description of the sample, development and use of tools, data collection procedure and statistical techniques used. Detailed analysis of data, its interpretation and discussion of results are presented in chapter four. Main findings of the study, its educational implications and suggestions for further research are presented in chapter five followed by Summary and Bibliography.

Scholarly guidance of Prof. D. S. Yadav, Deptt. of education, K.U. Kurukshetra has been invaluable. Likewise a debt of gratitude is acknowledged to my colleagues at University College of Education, K.U.K. for providing needed insight and constant support throughout the study. I also wish to express my appreciation for the Children and their parents for their willing participation and cooperation in the investigation. A deep sense of gratefulness to my Family and loving appreciation is expressed for Diksha and Bhaveya for letting me devote time and energy which should have been theirs.

Taruna Chaudhary Dhall

I
Introduction

Introduction

Each child is unique. This is obvious and astonishing. We remember it whenever we start to speak of children, school or education. The individual child is after all what the whole process of education is centered around. If we start from an individual child, most of us can quickly say what we most want for him, that he should grow and develop physically, emotionally and mentally so that he becomes an independent adult, the master and not the slave of circumstances. Mostly it is education that helps him to do this

Educational theories reveal that there is a general acceptance of significance of childhood experiences in the later educational growth of a person. Therefore a striking feature of contemporary educational thinking has been a growing concern about the effectiveness and efficiency of teaching-learning outcomes of a system of education which can be assessed in terms of student's school performance.

Viewing education as a means of development obviously means that we need to evolve certain educational models with the help of which changes in the form of educational growth can be brought about. Individual differences due to genetic influences are beyond the control of growth scientists and educationists. But identification of factors favourable for educational growth can help in developing such models and creating those conducive and wholesome experiences.

One of the most common beliefs is that the development of the child as considered from the point of view of competitive societies depends on what goes on in a school in terms of the curriculum transacted; through teaching-learning, other activities, student-teacher interactions etc. That is why, perhaps, most parents seek and want their children to be sent for better schooling, particularly to schools with the best available infrastructure and teachers. It is common knowledge that even in the same or similar school environments the school performance of children varies considerably. Such a situation calls for a search for factors other than school that create a difference or are associated with the performance of children at school. One naturally looks for the environments of vital significance.

It is now primarily for this reason that there is need to identify the determinants of educational growth from various aspects of life, which seem to guide an individual's performance in school. Identification of these determinants shall enable the educators to visualize what is of relevance to individual child's school performance.

Family Environment

The family is one of the primary groups of society concerned with face to face relationships. The term family is usually applied in both narrow and broad sense. In narrow sense it refers to the nuclear or immediate family, meaning parents and their children. In the broad sense it refers to the extended family, meaning not only the parents and children but also such other relatives as grandparents, uncles, aunts, cousins, nieces and nephews, that are either related by blood or marriage. From it stem the attitudes and behavior habits that set the pattern for social development and adjustment. The child in the family is the recipient of whatever constructive influences may result from the interrelations of his family with the social order.

Murdock (1949) suggests that the institution of family is universal and argues that four functions of family – sexual, economic, reproductive and educational are also universal. Family not only protects the child during its period of biological immunity, but is also an institution, which provides for the child's socialization and initial education. And one of the important aspects of learning process is the influence of family upon the child's ability to learn.

A child's physical, mental, and emotional potentialities reflect the characteristics of his forebearers. He inherits from his parents a differing degree of capacity to adjust to the demands of society. As he is stimulated by home influences that have their bases in parental nature and parental response to social pressures and directives, the child either is helped or is hindered in his effort towards whatever kind and extent of self-realization and social fulfillment he achieves through his participation in formal and informal educational experiences.

A child's earliest education is received in his family. It is here that his basic ideas and ideals are initiated, as well as the many attitudes towards himself and his associates that determine his later adjustment to school and other out-of- home situations. The economic status, attitudes and behavioural experiences of parents and family environment, all influence the child's behavior and attitudes, both directly and indirectly.

Environment has been defined in different ways. Murray (1938) proposed that environment should be defined by the kind of benefits or harms that it provides. Bloom (1949) defined the environment as the conditions, forces, and stimuli that influence the individual. He also suggested that "Such a view of the environment reduces it for analytical purpose to those aspects of the environment which are related to a particular characteristic or set of characteristics."

Accordingly if the development of a particular characteristic i.e. School Performance is to be understood, then it is necessary to identify those sub environments, which potentially are associated with school performance.

Family Environment and School Performance

Educational growth of the child and factors that influence its course are concerns that have long occupied the minds of psychologists, educators and parents. Two institutions that influence most directly the nature and quality of child's school performance are 'the family' and 'the school'. It is a plausible assumption that family prepares and reinforces the symbolic attribution required by the schooling and that schooling builds upon and elaborates the symbolic resources derived from family membership.

Family environment has often been conceptualized as status variables, such as socio-economic status. Broad static measures of socio-economic status typically are used without a detailed examination of the behaviours and experiences that may differ or remain constant across socio- economic levels.

Home environment and other family characteristics constitute one of the four most important factors that determine the level of achievement of a child in school.(Havighurst 1963). Another is the inborn ability of the child. Third one is the quality of schooling the child receives and the fourth factor is the child's self concept or aspiration level which grows out of family and school experiences. After several years of school experiences the child is able to determine how hard he or she shall work in school and towards what goals.

Nearly all families care about their children's school performance, but their knowledge of the system and their ability to work it to the advantage of their children varies. Stevenson and Baker (1987) through their study on family-school relation and the child's school performance, found that the extent to which parents were involved in school activities, such as parent-teacher organization and parent-teacher conferences, was positively related to children's school performance. Further, involvement was greater among parents of younger children and among more highly educated mothers.

More direct ways through which the family environment can influence school learning are through cognitive stimulation and assistance with schoolwork. MaCartney and Mouley (1992) observed that many of the home based intervention programs like reading stories to children, talking with them, providing toys and playing games-improve children's later performance in school and at times enhance their cognitive functioning.

Parents' provision of out of home experiences including taking children along for shopping, visiting zoos, museums and libraries can also stimulate cognitive development. These opportunities of informal learning about everyday world increase the fund of general information available to the child- a factor that has frequently been found to be predictive of skills in such areas as reading, languages and arts.

Beliefs and attitudes that parents hold are other family environment influences that affect a child's school learning and performance. Goodnow and Collins (1990) and Miller (1998) have documented how beliefs held by the family members affect children's development and how these in turn are related to their success at school.

Studies on socio-economic variables of family environment like parental occupation, parental income, level of parental education and prestige of the bread winner's occupation indicate that socio-economic status is positively, but not very strongly related to a variety of measures of scholastic ability and achievement. Further, there is evidence, though not entirely consistent that as children progress through school, the achievement gap between those from low socio-economic status homes to high socio-economic status homes tends to widen (Coleman et al. 1966, Fogelmen and Goldsten 1976).

Many investigators have tried to investigate the impact of other family environment influences besides socio-economic status on child's school performance. Fraser (1959) in an early study of the educational progress of Scottish secondary school students employed measures of cultural background (e.g. educational level of the parent, reading habits of parents), material and economic background (e.g. family income, number of rooms), motivational background (e.g. parental encouragement in school work) and emotional background (e.g.degree of harmony in the home, interest taken by parents in child's general welfare). The amount of variance in school progress accounted for by those home environment measures was much higher than the amount accounted for by measure of socio-economic status of family structures. Such findings have led to the importance of the impact of socio-psychological characteristics of family environment on school performance.

However considering the complexity of the interaction between parent and child, and other factors, that might affect the development in the child of a range of characteristics such as cognitive, attitudinal, and emotional relevant to scholastic performance, many investigators have been inspired to explore further and identify dynamic ongoing processes within the larger network of family interaction in place of static indices of socio-economic status as a means of improving understanding of the role of family in the cognitive and educational development of children (Bloom 1981, Marjoribanks, 1979).

Research evidence, on the role of particular process variable points out the importance of range of factors embracing expectation, inspiration, reinforcement and structure of the home. Findings of the studies, which have used such factors, indicate that within the area of scholastic achievement, family process variables are more closely related to general areas of achievement such as reading, rather than to more specialized areas such as science. Relationship between family process variable and scholastic ability and achievement have been found in several countries among different socio-economic and ethnic groupings, and in rural as well as in urban areas. Thus it can be said that there are differences in family environment within socio-economic and ethnic groups and that what is important for children's development is not so much what parents use in terms of socio-economic status than what they actually do (Kellaghan 1993).

Literature of such kind points towards a direction where it can be argued with conviction that support of school performance is possible in a range of families as parent contribute in different ways to their child's performance in school. The present investigation is an attempt to look into such related issues in the Indian context. Out of a variety of parent – child interactions only school focused parent – child interactions are proposed to be studied through five dimensions viz. Achievement Orientation, Cognitive Stimulation, Recreational Orientation, Home Structure and Language stimulation.

For the purpose of present study *Achievement Orientation* refers to the extent of Parental concern reflecting their belief and attitude, for child's education and other activities, Knowledge of progress of the child and provision of facilities for achieving educational goal.

Cognitive Stimulation refers to the encouragement and guidance to the child to indulge in thought provoking activities and opportunities made available to the child to develop thinking and imagination.

Recreational Orientation refers to the extent and content of interaction during indoor and out door activities, (purpose of) use of mass media and use of books, library or other such facilities.

Home Structure dimension of family environment is confined to degree of importance given by family members to the value of clear organizations and work habits, extent to which set rules and procedures are used to run family life and degree of help and support family members provide to each other.

Language stimulation addresses itself to the degree of importance shown to the quality of language used by parents / family members and opportunities made available to the child for expansion of vocabulary.

Justification of the Study

School performance is not an independent phenomenon, rather it is directly influenced by a number of factors, some of which are personal to the individual while many others are located in the environment in which the learning takes place i.e. school and family. Early beginnings to knowledge originate within the family, on a simple level in early years, and are then further built on in the school. Family sets the stage for interactions and learning at school later.

Families vary greatly in structure and functioning. Variations exist also in school and in children themselves. Given this diversity in families, there is a need to understand how children's experiences within the family contribute to their educational outcomes.

The family context often has been conceptualized as status variable such as socio-economic status. Research evidence indicates that socio-economic status is positively correlated with school performance but is not very significant. Broad static measures of Socio Economic Status typically are used, without a detailed examination of behavior and experiences that may differ or remain constant across socio-economic level.

Societal changes brought about as a result of technological advancement have had a dramatic impact on family environment in both developing and developed countries. This in turn has brought about a radical change in roles of different family members and parent-child interactions. A consensus is building, however that status variables are not as important as are family process variables in predicting academic success.

Since few researches in India have attempted to focus on the influence of changing family environment, there is need to study how different family process variables like cognitive stimulation, achievement orientation, recreational orientation, home structure and language stimulation, relate to School performance of Indian children.

Developmental psychologists have highlighted the importance of developmental status of the child. During the early formative years the child has two worlds-'Family and School'. Family environment influences individual differently according to the child's age. Variable affecting a six-year-old child may not necessarily operate in the same manner after the child has been in the school for several more years. Moreover as the child grows older and moves from being dependent on others to being independent, there is a decline in parent-child interaction. Thus, there is need to develop better insight into the influence of family environment on school performance of elementary school children as during this period the child is likely to interact more with his parents and other family members.

Since the acceptance of education as a constitutional right of children in the age group of 6-14 years, elementary education has been an area of concern for both, the educationist and the government of India. National Policy of Education – 1986, has underlined the importance of elementary education with attention being focussed on Universalzation of Elementary Education. Though the figures of enrolment have risen consistently, we still have a sizeable number of children outside the school stream. Universal enrolment is indeed a difficult problem, but even more so is the universal retention. Hence, there arises the need to study the influence of family environment on elementary school children as various advantageous and disadvantageous environments in the family and school influence the nature and quality of child's educational experiences. Therefore, no matter what we do inside the school, we can not make a significant impact without the informed support of the family.

Further the need of the study can be justified on the basis of findings of Balesky (1990) that parents rearing their children in a climate of affection and responsiveness, using clear and explicable rules, providing developmentally enhancing and autonomy granting environment, are more likely to have children with positive self concept who are emotionally stable, socially competent, well accepted by their peers, academically successful and intrinsically self responsible.

Thus research studies provided in the background do attach importance to the significance of family process variable on school performance. However in the Indian social-cultural context enough evidence regarding the relationship between Family Environment and School Performance, is lacking to make some genralizations. The investigation of such relationship is typically missing at the Elementary Level of education, which is considered to be a foundation period. Therefore, study of Family environment, As affecting the School Performance of Elementary School Children seems fully justified. It is in this background that the present study is undertaken, more specifically the folLowing is the problem undertaken.

Statement of the Problem " Impact of Family Environment on School Performance of Elementary School Children"

Operational Definition of the Terms used School Performance. School Performance refers to scholastic attainment of the child in Different subjects As an indicator of Cognitive and intellectual skills acquired during the course of teaching learning process. For the purpose of present study marks Obtained in class V are considered As School Performance.

Family Environment. For the present investigation Family Environmentrefers to School focussed Parent Child interactions with regard to Cognitive stimulation, Achievement Orientation, Recreational Orientation, home Structure and Language development.

Objectives of the Study

I. To develop and standardize a scale for measuring Family environment.

II. To study the relationship of School Performance of Elementary School Children with Family Environment and its dimension As Perceived by Children.

III. To study the relationship of School Performance of Elementary School Children with Family Environment and its dimensions As Perceived by Parents.

IV. To study the relationship between School Performance and Intelligence.

V. To study the relationship between School Performance and socio-Economic status.

VI. To study the impact of Family Environment on School Performance of Elementary School Children As brought out by School Performance Differentials at Different Levels of their Family Environment*As Perceived by Children.*

VII. To study the impact of Family Environment on School Performance of Elementary School Children As brought out by School Performance differentials at different levels of their Family Environment *as perceived by Parents.*

VIII. To study the impact of family environment on school performance of elementary school children, after isolating the influence of intelligence on their school performance, in terms of school performance differentials at different levels of their family environments and its dimension *as perceived by Children.*

IX. To study the impact of family environment on school performance of elementary school children, after isolating the influence of intelligence on their school performance, in terms of school performance differentials at different levels of their family environments and its dimension *as perceived by Parents.*

Hypotheses

I. There exists a significant positive relationship between School Performance of elementary school children and Family Environment *as perceived by Children.*

II. There exists a significant positive relationship between School Performance of elementary school children and Family Environment *as perceived by Parents.*

III. There exists a significant positive relationship between School Performance of elementary school children and their Intelligence..

IV. There exists a significant positive relationship between School Performance of elementary school children and their Socio-economic status.

V. If child experiences better family environment (school focused parent child interactions), then the child will exhibit higher school performance than the one, who experiences not so good family environment *as perceived by Children.*

VI. If child experiences better family environment (school focused parent child interactions), then the child will exhibit higher school performance than the one, who experiences not so good family environment *as perceived by Parents.*

VII. If child experiences better family environment (school focused parent child interactions), then the child will exhibit higher school performance than the one, *with similar intelligence,* who experiences not so good family environment *as perceived by Children.*

VIII. If child experiences better family environment (school focused parent child interactions), then the child will exhibit higher school performance than the one, *with similar intelligence,* who experiences not so good family environment *as perceived by Parents.*

Delimitation of the Study

The present study is presented within the following confinements:

The study is limited to class V students of D.A.V. Centenary Public Schools of Haryana.

The study is conducted only in the three districts of Haryana viz. Ambala, Karnal, and Kurukshetra.

The sample of the study is confined to all the class V students of four D.A.V. Centenary Public Schools selected randomly and their parents.

In the presented study Family Environment is delimited to five dimensions viz. Achievement Orientation, Cognitive Stimulation, Recreational Orientation, Home Structure and Language Stimulation.

2
Review of Related Literature

Review of related literature is an important research effort as it provides comprehensive understanding of what is known about the topic. The main functions of citing review of literature related to this study is to provide a basis for developing a framework, an insight into methodology and suggest operational definitions of concepts so as to work out a basis for interpretation of findings. Thus an attempt has been made in this chapter to review the studies related to this investigation.

Considering the prominence of family in the lives of most children, and the significance of scholastic performance for future life chances, it is not surprising that a vast amount of research now exists on the relationships between family background and school learning. Presumably, research indicates that the influence of the family on children's scholastic development is considerable. Literature is now emerging, suggesting that parent-child interaction in the home may influence behaviour in the school. Both school achievement and school functioning, particularly among young children, appear to be related to the relationship between parent and child.(Hess and Holloway, 1984; MacDonald & Parke, 1984.)

Bing (1963) in a study to investigate the effect of child rearing practices on development of differential cognitive abilities, used as sample, sixty mothers of fifth grader children. All of these children had similar total I.Q.scores and were divided by sex into high and low verbal groups. Data were obtained from questionnaires and from interviews with the mother as well as from observation of an "interaction situation" during which the mother engaged in various problem –solving activities with the child. Response on the retrospective questionnaire and interview indicated that mother of high verbal children provided more verbal stimulation in early childhood. These mothers also remembered more of child's early accomplishment, and were more critical of poor academic achievement. These mothers provided the child with more story books, and let him/her take a greater part in meal time conversation. The time spent in reading to the child by the father was associated with high verbal scores for girls only. Although no comparable association was found for reading time spent by the mothers with the children of either sex. In the observational situation mothers of children with high verbal ability generally provided more assistance voluntarily and, provided it sooner when requested by the child and pressured the child more for improvement.

Dave (1963), using a 63-item interview schedule as Wolf (1964) and apparently the same data, categorized the scales into five "Environmental Process Variables" that could be grouped to form an "Index of Educational Environment." The correlation of this overall "Index" with an "Educational Achievement Score" (composed of such areas as word knowledge, spelling, reading, and arithmetic computation) was found to be 80.

Bloom (1964), in an attempt to support a hypothesis of differential growth rate for human intellectual ability, reevaluated the data from longitudinal studies of the past four decades. He concluded that, in terms of intelligence measured at age 17, approximately 50% of the variance could be accounted for by age 4 so that as much intellectual growth is achieved between birth and four years of age, is achieved for the remaining thirteen years.

Wolf (1964) in an effort to relate parental influences to intelligence test performance of the child used data obtained from sixty fifth grade students and from interviews with their mothers. Those aspects of the home which were considered as most relevant to the development of general intelligence were incorporated as items in an interview schedule of 63 questions. The items were then used as a basis for rating on 13 scales designated as 'Environmental Process Characteristics'. The correlation of the total scores and the child's I.Q score was a striking 69. Individual correlation of the 13 scales with the intelligence test scores, the best relation were found for those scales dealing with the parents' intellectual expectation for the child, the amount of information that the mother had about the child's intellectual development, the opportunities provided for enlarging the child's vocabulary, the extent to which the parents created situations for learning in the home, and the extent of assistance given in learning situations related to school and nonschool activities.

Peaker (1967), in a large scale study carried out for Plowden report in England, contrasted home environment factors with primary- school

England, contrasted home environment factors with primary- school factors in predicting children's performance on standardized test of reading and Maths. Two aspects of home environment were assessed (a) parental attitude e.g. helpful and encouraging interest on the part of parents. (b) the material circumstances of the home e.g. parental income, physical amenities. Parental attitudes were found to account for more of variation in children's school achievement (28 per cent) than either the variation of home circumstances (20 Per cent) or variation in school (17 per cent).

Chatterji, Mukherjee and Banerjee (1972) conducted a study to investigate relation among scholastic achievement; SES and intellectual ability. They found that in all the three intellectual ability level, parental educational level is directly related to the scholastic achievement of their children.

Keeves (1972) collected data on Australian children, when they were in the final year of elementary school and in their first year of secondary school. Family context were assessed by three dimensions, that were categorized as structural, attitudinal and process. The three dimensions had moderate to strong association with mathematics and science achievement and low to modest concurrent validities with the children's attitudes to mathematics and science.

Marjoribanks (1972), developed and used a new measure of learning environment of the home, in order to examine the relationship between the environment of children and mental ability test performance. One hundred and eighty-five eleven years old boys and their parents formed the sample. Results revealed that environmental measure accounted for a large percentage of the variance in verbal number and total ability score and a moderate percentage of variance in reasoning ability score. For spatial ability the relationship with the environment was less definite. The environment measure accounted for more of the variance in the ability scores than did a set of social status indicators and family structure variables.

Kellaghan and Macnamara (1972) conducted a study to examine the 'relationship between verbal reasoning ability on one hand and sex, social class, family size and ordinal position in the family on the other side' ,on a representative sample of 11years old Irish children(N=500). In a separate analysis, regression coefficient of verbal reasoning score on social status and family size were found to be significant. In multiple regression analysis, social status, family size, and position in the family were all found to be significantly related to verbal reasoning score.

Walberg and Marjoribanks (1973) conducted a study on "Different Mental Abilities and Home Environment: A canonical analysis". A of stimulation in the family are related to the differential development of specific abilities. Although the first canonical variate revealed a strong link between general parental stimulation and global ability; the second variate showed that level of father's occupation and parental encouragement of activeness and language are related to higher verbal and reasoning scores, but lower number scores.

Bradley, Caldwell and Elardo, (1977) carried out an investigation with a purpose to compare environmental process measure and socio-economic status measure in terms of their relation with Stanford-Binet I.Q. at three years of age. Separate analyses were made for blacks and whites and for males and females. They found that the environment process measure predicts I.Q as well as a combination of process and status measures, where as there is some loss in predictive power when SES is used by itself (especially in case of blacks).

Krishnan (1977) investigated 180 students studying in classes fourth to tenth in a central school located at Tirupati in Andhra Pradesh. He found that parental education has positive influence on enhancing academic achievement of children.

Saini (1977) found that SES, as well as, the educational standard of parents has a significant effect on the academic achievement of art students at college level, but in case of science students, academic achievement is significantly related to the educational standards of parents but not to the SES of the family.

Sinha (1977) conducted a study on some social disadvantages and development of certain perceptual skills and reported that the magnitude of differences in performance between advantaged and disadvantage groups increases with age.

Misra (1978) in an experimental study of cognitive process as a function of prolonged deprivation found that a number of subjects hailing from a highly deprived background showed performance on a number of cognitive measures which was superior to the performance displayed by low deprivation group.

Grover (1979) conducted a study with an objective to find out the relationship between parental aspiration, certain personality traits and the school achievement of the children results of the study indicated some influence of aspiration of father and mother over children' academic achievement.

Salunke (1979) conducted a study on the first year college students of M.S. University, Baroda to see the relationship of the students' home environment with academic achievement. In this study cohesion, one of the dimensions of home environment was found to have correlation with academic achievement.

Homchaudhri (1980) conducted an analytical study of correlates of academic performance of college high achievers and found the emotional atmosphere of their homes to their liking. The low achievers found an absence of good environment at home on variable of cohesion.

White (1982) conducted a study to examine the relationship between SES and academic achievement and found that variation in home background has been found to account for an average of under 10 per cent of variance in a variety of measure of school performance in studies that used occupation as the family index.

Epstein (1983a, 1983b) while investigating the longitudinal effects of family-school-person: Interaction on students' outcome found that children from homes or classrooms affording greater opportunities for communication and decision making not only exhibited greater initiative and independence after entering high school but also received higher grades. Family process was considerably more powerful in producing changes than classroom procedures. The effects of family and school processes were greater than those attributable to SES or race.

Misra's (1983) review of Indian studies on 'Deprivation and Development' indicates that on the whole, the existing evidence does not clearly demonstrate any fundamental difference between so called 'deprived' and 'non-deprived' groups so far as general mental ability is concerned. However, they do show substantial differences in the degree of achievement, suggesting thereby the operation of some non-intellective factors as mediating variables, which critically determine the level of attainment.

Sarkar (1983) investigated the contribution of some home factors on children' scholastic achievement with an objective (I) to find the differences between high achievers and low achievers with respect to home factors like educational environment, income, property, special environment, social background, provision of facilities, parent-child relationship, home making role, punitive control and intelligence (ii) to obtain the multiple correlation and multiple regression equation between academic achievement and home environment. Findings of the study reveal a significant difference between high achievers and low achievers on the home variables – namely educational environment, income, spatial environment, social background provision of facilities and parent child relationship.

Seginer (1983) reviewed literature on personal educational expectation and children's academic achievement and found that in encouraging children to be aware of their own intellectual potential, parents may convey their aspiration and expectation for educational attainment and achievement. High achieving children tend to have families who hold high educational expectation.

Hess et. al.(1984) found that parents reading with their children and interacting with them verbally were related to children's reading performance. The family's provision of reading environment assessed by how often parents read to their children, was positively related to the reading performance of eleven years olds.

Hess and Holloway (1984) reviewed and analyzed results from students of preschool, primary, and middle-school children and identified five processes linking family and school achievement;

(i) verbal interaction between mother and children,
(ii) expectation of parents for achievement
(iii) positive affective relationship between parents and children,
(iv) parents' beliefs and attribution about the child,
(v) discipline and control strategies.

Lall (1984) carried out a study on child learning attitude, personal problems and personality factors as correlates of Academic Achievement. The main purpose of the study was (i) to investigate the relationship among child-rearing attitude of parents, youth problems and personality factors, such as locus of control, reinforcement, anxiety, extraversion and neuroticism and (ii) to study their relation with academic achievement. Findings of the study showed that protective attitude of parents was positively related to the academic success of boys.

Yusof (1984) conducted a study on the relationship between family communication self concept and academic achievement of adolescent in some schools of Petaling Java, Malaysia, and found that the Pearson's product moment correlation coefficient revealed a direct relationship between parent adolescent communication, i.e., the variable of expressiveness and adolescent academic achievement.

Jagannathan (1985) in a study on the effect of certain socio-psychological factors on the academic achievement of children studying in classes V & VIII, attempted to identify some of the personal, situational, and socio psychological variables affecting academic achievement. Finding of the study indicated a significant effect of home environment on academic achievement.

In a study by Maitra (1985) on affective correlates of the Gilfred underachievers, the findings revealed that home environment was found to be an important variable which could cause under achievement among the Gifted.

Griswold (1986) conducted a study on 'Family outing, Activity and Achievement among fourth graders in compensatory education funded school and found that (a)participation in family activities differed across racial groups and may be related to socioeconomic factors (b) achievement scores means were generally larger among activity participant than non participant regardless of racial grouping.

Studying the effects of home environment on the cognitive styles of students; Paul (1986) concluded that the factors of home environment, like recognition of the child; achievement, parental aspiration, forbearance for the child's wishes, parental affection, encouragement for initiative and freedom etc. had positive and significant correlation with each of the four modes of cognitive styles studied.

Using a representative sample of American households Stevenson and Baker (1987) examined the relationship between parental involvement in social activities on the child's school performance. They found out a significant positive correlation between the mother's education and the degree of parental involvement in school activities. Parents with more educational level were more involved in activities of the school such as parent teacher organization. parental involvement was related to school performance. Also, parents were more involved in school activities if the child was younger. The mother's educational level and age of the child were stronger predictors of parental involvement in schooling for boys than for girls.

Fehrman, Keith and Reimers (1987) on high school and beyond data set to examine the direct and indirect effect of parental involvement on high school grades. Results of their study revealed that parental involvement has important direct, positive effect on grades. Parental involvement also leads to increased time spent on homework; which in turn has a positive effect on grades. The effect of parental involvement on grades through TV time appeared negligible.

Trivedi (1987) designed an investigation to study the relationship between parental attitude, socio-economic status, feeling of security-insecurity and academic achievement of intermediate students with intelligence held constant. Finding of the study revealed that parental attitude was significantly related to academic achievement.

Vissar (1987) carried out an investigation with a purpose to study the relationship of parental attitudes and expectation to children's mathematics achievement behaviour and found that seventh and ninth graders' perception of parents' encouragement and expectation for mathematics were positively related to achievement in mathematics.

Chen and Uttal (1988) compared Chinese and U.S. mothers of first.

third and fifth graders. Both Chinese and U.S. mothers expected their children to earn similar scores on a mathematical test-about 80 to 85 of 100 points. U.S. mothers, however, said that they would be satisfied with scores 7 points lower than their expected scores. The score that would satisfy Chinese mothers was 10 points higher than their expectation. Thus Chinese mothers appeared to have higher standard for their children scored higher on mathematics achievement.

Wood; Chapin and Hannah (1988) found that high achieving high school students rated their families significantly high on scales of achievement orientation and intellectual/cultural orientation than did low achievers.

Lin and Atkin (1989) conducted a study on parental mediation and rule making for adolescents' use of television and VCRs. They found that for seventh and tenth graders, parents rule about television viewing and parents' mediation or enforcement of television viewing standards were positively associated with standard grades.

Bevli (1990), in a study examined the effect of home school and individual variables on the cognitive development of Indian children coming from disadvantaged environment and found that SES of parents; facilities for play; school facilities; school fees; intelligence and ethical discrimination are found to be highly correlated with the concept of numbers, length, area and volume. This concept also shows significant ($p<0.01$) relationship with the achievement test of arithmetic and language.

Mishra and Tiwari (1990) conducted a study to understand cognitive development of children from an ecological perspective. They found that environmental influences are multi-faceted and depend upon the specific nature of cognitive skill as well as the developmental stage of children.

Muralidharan (1990) investigated the effects of parent–related, school related, child related variables, SES and facilities provided at home and achievement of children in primary school. The findings showed that almost all home variables-maternal behaviors, attitudes as well as facilities have a significant relationship with the child's achievement in school .In contrast school variable did not prove to have much effect on child's achievement. The socio-economic status variables, as expected proved to be constantly having a significant impact. Among the child-related variables, the child's independence was found to affect his achievement.

Wentzel, Feldman and Weinbergee (1991) carried out an investigation with a purpose to study the mediational role of socio-emotional adjustment on academic achievement on sixth graders. They found that grade point average was negatively related to mother's and father's harsh and inconsistent discipline and was positively related to students' self –

restraint.

Bhatnagar and Sharma (1992) carried out an investigation to study the relationship between parental education and academic achievement of students. The sample consisted of 185, ninth, tenth, eleventh class students in semi rural setting in Rajasthan. Results indicated that the children whose parents attended school performed at a significantly higher academic level than others. Parent's education appeared to be related to the academic achievement of students.

Cherian (1992) in a study investigated the relationship between parental aspiration and academic achievement and found that parental aspiration for their children's' educational attainment were positively related to adolescents' grades in a sample of urban and rural black Xhosa-speaking monogamous and polygamous families in Transkeiv, South Africa.

Crimm (1992) conducted a meta- analytical study on parent involvement and academic achievement. The purpose of the study was to examine the existing body of literature and through the case of meta-analysis determine the effect of parent involvement on academic achievement. A collection of 57 quantitative studies was reviewed and the meta-analysis of those studies produced an effect size, which indicated that parent involvement has a positive impact upon a child's academic success. The analysis of the sorted studies revealed that elementary students (grade-3 to 5) benefit the most from parent involvement, home visits have the greatest impact, and reading improves the most as a result of parent involvement.

Mullar (1993) in an analysis of family resources available to the child found that parents' talking with their children about current school experiences was positively associated with achievement test scores and with grades. In addition parents talking with eighth graders about high school plans was positively associated with grades.

Anderson (1994) studied the effect of parental involvement on academic achievement. The purpose of the study was to determine if involving their parents in the educational process could increase the achievement level of secondary school students. Subjects were randomly selected similar in age, grade level, range of achievement level, types of courses taken and economic status. The evidence gathered supported the position that those students whose parents displayed some marked degree of participation in school-related activities achieved significantly more.

Grolnick and Slowiaczek (1994) conducted a study on 300, 11-14 years old children and their teachers, to examine multidimensional conceptualization of parent involvement in schooling. Factors analysis of a set of parent involvement measures supported the three dimensions of parent involvement; behaviour, intellectual/cognitive and personal. Path analyses revealed indirect effects of mother behaviour and intellectual/cognitive involvement in school performance through perceived competence and control understanding, and indirect effect of father behaviour on school performance through perceived competence.

Whang and Hancock (1994) in a study compared motivation and mathematics achievement between Asian American and non-Asian students. They reported that Asian American fourth-, fifth-, and sixth grade students performed significantly higher than white students on mathematics achievement test, but the Asian American students were less likely to believe they were meeting their parents expectation, which presumably were higher than those of white parents.

Chilampikunnel (1995), studied parental involvement and students performance and self-esteem in sub-urban and city parochial elementary (k-6) schools. The participants of the study included 317 elementary school children from three catholic schools in Westchester country and three from the Bronx in New York City. The major findings indicated that parent involvement in school-home communication, and parental attitude towards school had a significant correlation with children's performance, attendance and self-esteem. The study also found that students from Westchester country catholic schools had a significantly higher self-esteem and attendance than those from the Bronx.

Addington (1997), studied effects of parental involvement on mathematics achievement at eighth, tenth and twelfth graders. The results suggest that parental involvement in students academic lives is indeed a powerful influence on students' mathematics achievement at eighth, tenth and twelfth grade. Findings also suggest that conscious effort to communicate parental aspiration for their child's future educational attainment can act as a useful tool to help increase mathematics achievement at secondary school level.

Khare (1997) conducted a study to know the influence of the home environment on the creative writing ability of school children. Main objective of the study were (i) to study the influence of home environment factors on the creative writing in Hindi language. (ii) to study whether the difference in learning environment of home have any association with difference in creativity (iii) Whether the creative writing abilities are affected by the interactions of home learning environment with other personal social variables namely age, sex of the child. Results of the study revealed that there is (i) no significant relationship between learning environmental and creative writing ability of the different sub-samples. But correlation for the total sample has been found to be significant at 0.05 level. (ii) Significant gender differences on the creative writing (iii) A 2x2x2 design ANOVA for creative writing ability scores contribute towards variation in the creative ability of students.

Zhao (1997), studied social class and differences in parental expectation and involvement in education: a study of two school in urban Shangai. Forty-eight families including children and parents participated in this research. Data collection was completed through interviews and observations. Interview protocols were prepared and used for parents and students respectively. The findings of the research indicate that parental expectation is closely related with parents' educational level, while parental involvement in education is determined by more than one factor and parents' SES is the most important.

Using national data Trusty (1998) investigated the influence of family and parenting variables as expectation regarding education among late adolescents. Results of the study revealed that (a) SES was the strongest predictor of late adolescents educational expectation; (b) parents' attendance at extracurricular activities and adolescents' perception of parents personal educational support seem to influence adolescents educational expectation, above and beyond the effect of SES.

Moline (1999) studied the parental involvement, student achievement link, to provide a scholarly basis for justifying and implementing parental involvement programs that produce significant and long-lasting effects on child's academic outcomes. In doing so, educational institutions can expect to reap the rewards of improved student achievement. Research reveals that parental involvement at home and involvement at school are not equally important to children's learning. The home environment is among the most important influences on academic achievement, parents, teachers and child development. Parents of high achieving students had a distinct style of interacting with their children, and created emotionally supportive home environments.

Effect of Home Environment on Intelligence and Educational aspiration of senior higher secondary school students was studies by Thakur (2001). Objectives of the study were to find out the correlation between educational aspiration and intelligence, inter-relationship between Home Environment and Educational Aspiration and Intelligence. Relationship between Intelligence and Socio-Economic Status and Relationship between Socio-Economic Status and Educational Aspirations. Results reveal that all the dependent variables have effect on the independent variable, with effect of home environment on Intelligence and educational aspirations. Subjects who have good home environment probably possess a likelihood of securing better scores on intelligence and educational aspiration scale.

Literature cited above indicates that a child's performance in school has been studied in relation to a number of variables like age, residential areas, education and occupation of parents, their beliefs, expectations, social class etc. A significant indicator of this review is that the attention of the researchers in the west has been shifted from gross status variables to environmental process variables. (Dave, 1963; Wolf,1964; Bloom, 1964; Moss,1974; Caldwell & Bradly, 1978 and Marjoribank 1979). Increasingly greater attention is being paid to the analysis of home environment variables in relation to cognitive development. However, research evidence of such kind is typically lacking in the indian context.

Indian studies of environmental influence on cognitive development have largely been concerned with static characteristics and more so with disadvantaged rather than development under normal conditions. (Sarkar, 1983; Misra, 1978 and Sinha, 1979). These studies do help in understanding the magnitude of effect but are at a loss in explaining the dynamic psychological process as influencing school performance except in a very limited sense.

Therefore, present study is aimed at exploring the impact of specific school-focussed parent child interaction in relation to school performance of elementary school children.

3

Plan and Procedure

Introduction

In the previous chapter the development of the problem for the present study has been traced in the light of theoretical and research background. This chapter is devoted to the method and procedure followed in the investigation. Therefore, an attempt has been made to provide methodological plan and procedure followed under the following sub-heads.

Methodology
Sampling
Tools Used
Procedure for data collection
Statistical techniques used

Methodology

There are several methods of conducting research. Choice of method of research is determined by the nature of the problem. The present study attempts to study the impact of family environment on the school performance of elementary school children. It is obvious that the impact of family environment cannot be studied in any artificial setting, nor is it desirable to do so. In the present study the descriptive method of research is found to be the most appropriate one as Parent-child interactions as they exist can effectively be studied.

The descriptive method of research has been the most popular and widely used research method in sociology and education, because of the ease of this method. Information can be gathered by a questionnaire or interview schedule. Although the descriptive method of research is relatively less sophisticated in comparison to the experimental method. It has its own advantages. The descriptive studies are more than mere collection of data. They involve measurement, classification, analysis, comparisons and interpretation. Such research seeks to find answers to questions through the analysis of variable relationships.

Descriptive studies investigate the phenomenon in their natural setting. Descriptive research is designed to obtain pertinent and precise information concerning the current status or phenomenon and wherever possible to draw valid general conclusions from the facts discovered. School focussed parent child interactions cannot be studied in controlled situations, so survey method is adopted for the present study.

The present study was designed to investigate the impact of school focussed parent child interactions on the school performance of elementary school children. For this purpose a three phased study was planned for the present investigation. At the first phase the degree of association of School Performance of elementary school children with and their Family Environment, Intelligence and Socio-economic status is to be obtained.

At the second phase an attempt was made to make up deficiencies of correlational studies in that they give no idea regarding causation. This could be possible by studying the differences in school performance of elementary school children at three levels of family environment, i.e., Enriched, Moderate and Low. This grouping of respondents was done by applying the formula Mean ± ½ S.D. to the score value.

Influence of intelligence on the school performance of a child is well documented. Therefore, at the third phase an effort was made to isolate the influence of intelligence on the school performance of elementary school children. This was ensured by studying the differences in school performance of elementary school children belonging to Similar Intelligence groups i.e. high, moderate and low at three levels of family environment. This grouping of respondents was done by applying the formula Mean ± ½ S.D. to the score value of their intelligence.

Sampling

Sampling refers to the methods used to select a given number of people or things from a population. The strategy of selecting a sample influences the quality of data and the inferences that can be drawn from it. Within all approaches to research, researchers use sampling for very practical reasons. In most research studies, it is just not feasible to collect data from every individual in a setting or population. Therefore, sampling makes it possible to draw valid generalizations by studying a relatively small proportion of the population selected for observation and analysis.

The present study aims at investigating the impact of family environment on school performance of elementary school children. Keeping in view the delimitation of the study, population of the present study consisted of class V students of DAV Public School of Haryana and their parents. The sample was selected phase wise.

Selection of School

For the selection of the schools the investigator first of all purposively selected three districts namely Ambala, Karnal and Kurukshetra out of the 19 districts of Haryana. Out of a large number of schools i.e. Government schools ,Government aided schools and private schools, the criterion adopted for the selection of school was to isolate the influence of school environment on school performance. Accordingly four D.A.V. Centenary Public Schools managed by DAV College managing committee, Chitragupt Road, New Delhi were selected randomly. The selected schools were (i) D.A.V. Centenary Public School Ambala City, (ii) D.A.V. Centenary Public School, Karnal (iii) D.A.V. Centenary Public School, Kurukshetra (iv) D.A.V. Centenary Public School, Shahabad. These schools run by the DAV management have the provision of common board examinations for V & VIII class, ensuring uniform standards of evaluation in the entire region. Selection of these schools of similar nature was guided by another important consideration – the uniformity of policies and programmes followed in these institutions under the same management.

Selection of Respondents

For the purpose of collecting data on the variables under investigation, all the students of class V, present on the day in their respective school and their parents were taken as samples. Thus 405 elementary school children belonging to class V of DAV schools and 405 parents of these children constituted the sample of the study. However because of reckless attempts and incomplete responses from the respondents, finally 185 students and 175 parents were considered for the analyses of results.

Tools Used

The following tools were used for collecting the required data.

- Family environment scale for Children developed and standardized by the researcher.
- Family Environment Scale for Parents - developed and standardized by the researcher.
- Non Verbal Intelligence test developed by Navodaya Vidayalya Samiti and adapted by the researcher.
- Socio Economic Status Inventory prepared by the researcher.

Construction of Family Environment Scale

The family environment scale was developed with a view to have an instrument to measure school focussed parent-child interactions as perceived by children and parents. Initially a pilot survey was conducted for this purpose.

Pilot Survey

A pilot survey was conducted by visiting a number of schools and homes in order to get an insight into the type of school focussed parent child interactions within the family. It was decided to carry out informal interviews with parents, teachers, students and experts in the field. It was considered essential to ask them about the type of parent child interactions, which they felt, have a positive influence on a child's school performance. They were told that the interviewer wished to know what kind of interest parents took in their child's education and how they expressed it. The interviewer was particularly interested in knowing the points these people emphasized and were particular about. In other words, interviews were conducted to know what experts believed in general and what the parents do in particular. Initially 20 such interviews were conducted in the university campus area of Kurukshetra. The initial responses of teachers, students, their parents and experts in the field, contacted during the pilot survey yielded significant information and an initial pool of items was obtained. Additional items were adapted from other existing tools.

The pilot survey thus enabled the researcher in discerning information from the actual field setting and helped in exploring the diverse facts of the problem for preparing the tools for study.

Family Environment Scale for Children

A Child and a Parent may perceive the environment within the family differently. Therefore in order to know their responses individually, two forms of family environment scales were developed one for the Children and other for the parents.

Writing of Statements Family Environment Scale (FES) for Children

On the basis of the study of literature, information gathered during the pilot survey and personal experiences, an exhaustive list of items pertaining to school focussed parent child interactions was prepared. While framing the statements for this purpose some suggestion given by Cannal and Kahn (1970) regarding preparation of such a tool, e.g., frame of reference; level of information; social acceptance; form of statement; single item statement etc. were considered. The final list of items thus prepared was given to the language expert for vetting. The preliminary draft of the tool so constructed was given to some faculty members of Kurukshetra University for their expert comments. The same was modified in the light of their suggestions. The first draft was given to the language expert for vetting and it was then considered fir for try-out.

Try-out and revision

The first draft of the family environment scale thus prepared was given to a small group of students concerned for the purpose of removing any ambiguities and to see if the items properly communicated what the same were intended to. This initial try-out led to the further revision and refinement of the tool for its effectiveness.

After the initial try-out and the revision the first draft of the tool was administered to a large group consisting of 47 students. In the light of their responses the necessary modifications were made and the first draft of the tool was prepared for the purpose of data collection. The detailed procedure adopted in the construction of the tool is given in Appendix-1. Here it may briefly be mentioned that first draft of Family environment scale consisted of 82 items. These belonged to five dimensions of Family environment viz. Achievement Orientation; Cognitive Stimulation; Recreational Orientation; Home Structure and Language Stimulation. Table 3.1 below provides dimension-wise items of the scale thus developed.

Table 3.1

Distribution of Items on Various Dimensions of First Draft of Family Environment Scale (Fes) For Children

S.No.	*Dimension of FES*	*numbers of Items*
1.	Achievement orientation	(13)
2.	Cognitive stimulation	(19)
3.	Recreational orientation	(18)
4.	Home structure	(19)
5.	Language stimulation	(13)

The Family Environment Scale for Children consisting of 82 items was given to 405 students to obtain their responses for the purpose of item analysis. The item analysis of the scales was done by computing the discrimination value. Besides this in order to ensure a degree of homogeneity in the tool, item-total score correlation for each dimension was calculated.

Those items that did not fulfil any of the criteria i.e. discrimination value and degree of homogeneity were eliminated. The items thus selected constituted the final form of the scale. The test-retest, split half reliability and validity of the final tool was worked out and after adopting the proper procedure for its construction the final form of the tool consisted of 70 items. Table 3.2 below provides distribution of items on various dimensions of final form of family environment scale for children, selected after item analysis.

Table 3.2
Distribution of Items on Various Dimensions of Final form of Family Environment Scale for Children

S.No.	*Dimension*	*Number of Items*
1.	Achievement Orientation	10
2.	Cognitive Stimulation	16
3.	Recreational Orientation	15
4.	Home Structure	16
5.	Language Stimulation	13

Scoring

Scoring procedure of family environment scale was very simple and objective. It was the same for both the forms. Each item had three responses representing the kind of interaction in the family viz. a) indifferent; b) moderate; c) stimulating. a, b, and c, were scored as 0, 1, and 2 respectively.

Family Environment Scale for Parents

A procedure similar to the one followed for developing a scale for children was followed for the construction of family environment scale for the parents and all the items were selected. Intended meaning and contents of each of the statements was kept the same. However the statements were worded as per the need.

Non Verbal Test of Intelligence

A non-verbal test of intelligence developed by Navodaya Vidyalaya Samiti was adapted by the researcher in the present study, for measuring intelligence of the subjects. The test consisted of 60 items divided into four sections of 15 items each. Each section was preceded by printed instructions to be followed in responding all the 15 items in each section. Time allotted for the test was one hour. Subjects were required to tick one of the four alternative responses provided for each item as only one of them was correct. Every correct response was scored as 1 and incorrect as 0. Thus a subject could score from 0 to 60.

This test was given to 453 students of class V of different primary school. For the purpose of item analysis, at first the data obtained from all the subjects on non-verbal test of intelligence was arranged in ascending order. The upper and lower group of 122 each (27 per cent of the subjects) then formed the criterion group, in terms of which the individual items were analyzed. Proportion of the two groups that answered the items correctly was computed to find out the discrimination indices for each item. Items with value less than 0.40 were dropped from the final form of the test. Results of item discrimination index of 60 items revealed that 10 items did not fulfil the said criterion i.e. their value was less than 0.40. Discrimination value of each item is presented in Appendix- VII. Thus item no. 9, 10, 11, 22, 28, 29, 35, 36, 44 and 55 were not considered for the purpose of scoring. Thus after adopting the proper procedure for item analysis the final form consisted of 50 items. Accordingly a subject could score a minimum of 0 and maximum of 50. The test retest reliability of non verbal test of intelligence was 0.89 and split half reliability calculated by using Spearman-Brown prophecy formula and the reliability coefficient of the whole test came out to be 0.863.

Socio Economic Status Inventory

On the basis of study of literature, information gathered during discussion with experts and personal experiences a number of items concerning static factors related to the individual and his family background were prepared to develop a socio economis status inventory.

The list of items thus prepared was given to language experts for vetting and to some faculty members of Kurukshetra university for their expert comments. Items were modified in the light of their suggestions. The inventory thus prepared was given to a small group of students, for the purpose of removing any ambiguities and to ensure that each item properly communicated what it intended to. The responses thus received enabled the researcher to further revise and refine the inventory for its effectiveness and thus the final shape to the inventory was given by the investigator to measure socio economic status of children. Inventory contained items covering the following areas: -

§ Personal information about the subjects such as name, age, sex, name of the school , residential address etc.

§ Information about educational level and occupation of mother and father

§ Information regarding the kind of availability of means of (exposure to) mass media like news paper, magazine radio, audio system, television, computer, internet etc.

§ Facilities for learning at home like provision of study room or corner.

§ A checklist of material possession or household amenities likes car, scooter, cycle refrigerator cooler airconditioner etc.

All the items were framed in simple language so that the respondents could understand the same easily. Sum of scores on all the items was taken as socio economic score of the children.

Procedure for Data Collection

After finalizing the sample tools and techniques for data collection the investigator contacted the heads of schools. She discussed in detail the purpose of investigation with the heads of respective schools and sought permission to collect data from class V students of the school. Authorities were kind and cooperative enough to provide suitable space where in the tools could be administered to the subjects.

The data was collected by the investigator herself in small groups of 30-35 subjects at a time. The help of class teacher was sought in seeking cooperation from the respondents. The data was collected in two phases. In the first phase, after apprising the students about the nature and purpose of the study, family environment scale for children was administered to all the students of class V present on that day in the school. Usual requirement for proper test administration were ensured. In order to establish good rapport; the investigator made introductory remarks approp' ate to the situation.

Respondents were apprised that their results will be kept strictly confidential. Instructions were read aloud to the subject while they followed them in the test booklets. After ensuring, that instruction were clear to all respondents; they were asked to open the test booklet and start responding. Simple clarification of word meanings, if any, were given on request but care was taken not to influence the direction of the respondents' responses. In the end, each subject was thanked by the investigator.

For parents' responses, test booklet were sent to the parents of student respondents, with the help of the class teachers. Students were requested to get it filled from their parents and return the same within three days. Investigator collected the same from school after the given period.

In the second phase, all the students whose parents had returned family environment scale were administered intelligence test and Socio-economic status inventory. This process was repeated for two days in each school.

In the third phase, marks obtained by the students in their class V examination, were collected from authorities of respective schools.

Statistical Techniques Used

The data was analysed with the help of following statistical technique:

1. Coefficient of correlation to find out the relationship.
2. 't-ratio' to find out the differentials.

4
Analysis, Interpretation, and Discussion of Result

Introduction

It has been argued in the background of the study that school performance is not an independent phenomenon, rather it can reasonably be conceived as the one that is modifiable by variation in the environment. This phenomenon is also developmental in nature. As such, there are a number of factors, namely, personal characteristics (cognitive as well as non-cognitive), school environment, and family environment, which have direct bearing on the school performance of the child. Keeping in view the requirements of the study the next step was to analyze and interpret the data in the light of the objectives and hypotheses of the study. As stated in chapter one, the main purpose of the present study is to investigate the "Impact of Family Environment on school performance of elementary school children." In order to find out the impact of children's perception of family environment as well as parents' perception of family environment on School Performance of elementary school children, the results have been analyzed, interpreted and discussed in three sections.

Section-I deals with school performance of elementary school children in relation to their Family Environment, Intelligence and Socio-Economic Status as brought out in terms of correlates.

Section-II deals with the impact of Family Environment on the School Performance of elementary school children. For this purpose, school performance differentials will be examined at different levels of their Family Environment.

Section-III will deal with an in-depth analysis as brought out by school performance differentials of elementary school children belonging to *similar intelligence groups* at different levels of their Family Environment.

School Performance of Elementary School Children Relation to their Family Environment, Intelligence and Socio-Economic Status

This section of the study deals with the relationship of school performance of elementary school children with their Over all Family Environment and its different dimensions viz. Achievement Orientation, Cognitive Stimulation, Recreational Orientation, Home Structure and Language Stimulation, as perceived by Children and Parents. Further it also provides the Intelligence and Socio-economic status correlates of school performance of these children.

School Performance of Elementary School Children in Relation to Children's Perception of Family Environment

This part of the section deals with the relationship of school performance of elementary school children with their Family Environment, as perceived by *Children*. Coefficients of correlation between school performance of elementary school children and their Overall Family Environment and its five dimensions (as perceived by Children) are given below:

Table 4.1

Coefficients of Correlation Between School Performance of Elementary School Children and their Overall Family Environment and its Five Dimensions (As Perceived by Children) N = 185

Variable	*Coefficient of Correlation*	*Level of Significance*
Overall Family Environment	0.528	0.01
Achievement Orientation	0.346	0.01
Cognitive stimulation	0.424	0.01
Recreational Orientation	0.424	0.01
Home Structure	0.460	0.01
Language Stimulation	0.529	0.01

It can be observed from Table 4.1 that coefficient of correlation between school performance of elementary school children and overall family environment is 0.528, which is significant at 0.01 level. This indicates that there is high positive correlation between overall family environment and school performance of elementary school children.

It can further be observed from Table 4.1 and that coefficients of correlation between school performance of elementary school children and different dimensions of family environment viz., achievement orientation, cognitive stimulation, recreational orientation, home structure, and language stimulation have come out as 0.346, 0.424, 0.424, 0.460, 0.529 respectively. All these coefficients are significant at .01 level, indicating high positive relationship between different dimensions of Family Environment and School performance of elementary school children. Out of all these coefficients Language stimulation has been found to develop a still greater relationship with school performance in comparison to other dimensions of Family Environment (as perceived by children). Results reveal a significant positive relationship of school performance of elementary school children with their Overall Family Environment and its five dimensions. It indicates a close association between School Performance of elementary school children and their Family Environment.

Thus, the first hypothesis of the present study that 'there exists a significant positive relationship between School performance of elementary school children and their Family Environment (as perceived by children)' is retained with respect to Overall Family Environment as well as its five dimensions viz. Achievement orientation, Cognitive stimulation, Recreational orientation, Home structure and Language stimulation.

School Performance of Elementary School Children in Relation to *Parents' Perception* of Family Environment

This part of the section deals with the relationship of School Performance of elementary school children with their Family Environment, as perceived by *Parents*. Coefficients of correlation between school performance of elementary school children and their Overall Family Environment and its five dimensions (as perceived by Parents) are given below:

Table 4.2 show that coefficient of correlation between and school performance of elementary school children and their and overall family environment is 0.503, which is significant at 0.01. This indicates that there is high positive correlation between overall family environment and school performance of elementary school children.

Table 4.2

Coefficients of Correlation Between School Performance Elementary School Children and their Overall Family Environment and its Five Dimensions (As Perceived by Parents) N = 175

Variable	*Coefficient of Correlation*	*Level of Significance*
Overall Family Environment	0.503	0.01
Achievement Orientation	0.475	0.01
Cognitive stimulation	0.473	0.01
Recreational Orientation	0.384	0.01
Home Structure	0.416	0.01
Language Stimulation	0.350	0.01

It can also be seen from Table 4.2 that coefficients of correlation between school performance of elementary school children and different dimensions of family environment viz., Achievement orientation, Cognitive stimulation, Recreational orientation, Home structure, and Language stimulation, have come out to be 0.475, 0.473, 0.384, 0.416, 0.350 respectively. All these coefficients are significant at 0.01 level, indicating high positive relationship between different dimensions of family environment and school performance of elementary school children. Achievement orientation and cognitive stimulation have been found to develop relatively higher the highest relationship with school performance in comparison to other dimensions of family environment (as perceived by Parents). Results reveal that family environment and its five dimensions reveal a significant positive relationship with School performance of elementary school children. It indicates a close association between School Performance of elementary school children and their Family Environment.

Thus the second hypothesis of the present study that there exists a significant positive relationship between School performance of elementary school children and Family Environment (as perceived by Parents) is retained with respect to Overall Family Environment as well as it's five dimensions viz. Achievement orientation, Cognitive stimulation, Recreational orientation, Home structure, and Language stimulation.

School Performance of Elementary School Children in Relation to their Intelligence

Coefficient of correlation between school performance of elementary school children and their intelligence as measured by Non-Verbal test of intelligence is given below:

Table 4.3
Coefficients of Correlation Between School Performance of Elementary School Children and their Intelligence, N =185

Variable	*Coefficient of Correlation*	*Level of Significance*
Intelligence	0.395	0.01

It can be observed from table 4.3 that coefficient of correlation between school performance and intelligence is 0.395 which is significant at 0.01 level. This indicates that there is high positive relationship between school performance of elementary school children and their intelligence.

Therefore, Hy3 of the present study that there exists a significant positive relationship between School Performance of elementary school children and their Intelligence is retained.

Table 4.4
Coefficients of Correlation Between School Performance of Elementary School Children and their Socio-Economic Status, N =185

Variable	*Coefficient of Correlation*	*Level of Significance*
Socio-Economic Status	0.139	NS

It can be observed from table 4.4 that coefficient of correlation between school performance and Socio-Economic status is 0.139 which is less than the tabie value (0.1443) and as such not significant even at 0.05 level. This indicates that there is no significant relationship between school performance of elementary school children and their socio-economic status.

Therefore, Hy4 of the present study that there exists a significant positive relationship between School Performance of elementary school children and their Socio-Economic status is not retained.

Impact of Family Environment on School Performance of Elementary School Children

In this section an attempt has been made to study the impact of family environment (as perceived by Children and Parents) on the school performance of elementary school children. For this purpose, *school performance differentials* were examined at different level of family environment. For an in-depth analysis school performance differentials were also examined at different levels of all the five dimensions of family environment, as perceived by Children and Parents. For this purpose subject have been classified into three groups, i.e., Enriched family environment, Moderate family environment and Low family environment groups by adopting the criterion of Mean ± ½ SD to the score value of overall family environment and its five dimension as perceived by children and parents. Classification of subjects into three groups on basis of score value of family environment as perceived by children and parents is presented in table 4.5 and 4.6.

Table 4.5

Classification of Subjects into Three Groups in Terms of Their Score Value on Overall Family Environment and Its Five Dimension (as perceived by children) N = 185

Variable	*Mean*	*S.D*	*Enriched family environment Group*	*Moderate family environment Group*	*Low family environment Group*
Overall family environment	113.45	13.52	120 and above	between 120 and 107	107 and below
Achievement Orientation	18.07	1.71	19 and above	between 19 and 17	17 and below
Cognitive Stimulation	25.67	3.84	28 and above	between 28 and 24	24 and below
Recreational Orientation	23.16	3.38	25 and above	between 25 and 21	21 and below
Home Structure	26.19	3.63	28 and above	between 28 and 24	24 and below
Language Stimulation	20.36	3.43	22 and above	between 22 and 19	19 and below

Table 4.6
Classification of Subjects into Three Groups in Terms of Their Score Value on Overall Family Environment and Its Five Dimension (as perceived by parents) N = 175

Variable	*Mean*	*S.D*	*Enriched family environment*	*Moderate family environment*	*Low family environment*
Overall family enviro-nment	114.3	12.8	121 and above	between 121 and 108	108 and below
Achiev-ement Orient-ation	18.0	1.8	19 and above	between 19 and 17	17 and below
Cogni-tive Sti-mulation	25.9	3.8	28 and above	between 28 and 24	24 and below
Recrea-tional Orien-tation	23.5	3.5	25 and above	between 25 and 22	22 and below
Home Struc-ture	26.8	3.3	28 and above	between 28 and 25	25 and below
Langu-age Stim-ulation	20.2	3.0	22 and above	between 22 and 19	19 and below

School Performance Differentials in Elementary School Children at Different Level of Family Environment (as Perceived by Children)

School performance differentials of elementary school children at different levels of their overall family environment and its five dimensions, as perceived by *Children* are presented below in tables 4.7 to 4.12.

Table 4.7
Significance of Difference in the Mean School Performance Scores of Elementary School Children at Different Level of *Overall Family Environment* (As Perceived by Children)

Groups	*N*	*M*	*S.D*	*t-ratio*	*Level of significance*
Enriched overall family environment	69	89.261	10.039		
Vs				9.3967	0.01
Low overall family environment	61	68.754	14.193		
Enriched overall family environment	69	89.261	10.039		
Vs				5.5905	0.01
Moderate overall family environment	55	74.564	17.315		
Moderate overall family environment	55	74.564	17.315		
Vs				1.9636	0.05
Low overall family environment	61	68.754	14.193		

Table 4.7 shows that the mean school performance score of enriched overall family environment group is 89.261 and that of low overall family environment group is 68.754, with SDs 10.039 and 14.193 respectively. The obtained 't' value is 9.3967 and this is found to be significant at .01 level. Thus, it can be inferred that the two groups differ significantly in their school performance. The mean school performance score of enriched overall family environment group is higher than that of low overall family environment group. It indicates that children with enriched overall family environment are found to have better school performance than those belonging to low overall family environment group.

Table 4.7 further shows that the mean school performance score of enriched overall family environment group is 89.261 and that of moderate overall family environment group is 74.564, with SDs 10.039 and 17.315 respectively. The obtained 't'-value is found to be significant at 0.01 level of significance. It implies that the two groups differ significantly in their school performance. The mean school performance score of enriched overall family environment group is higher than the moderate overall family environment group. It suggests that children experiencing enriched overall family environment are found to have better school performance in comparison to those experiencing moderate overall family environment.

It can also be seen from the above table that mean school performance score of moderate overall family environment group is 74.564 and that of low overall family environment group is 68.754, with SDs 17.315 and 14.193 respectively. The obtained 't' value is 1.9636, and this is found to be significant at 0.05 level of significance. It means that the two groups differ significantly in their school performance. The mean school performance of moderate overall family environment group is higher than that of low overall family environment group. It means that children experiencing moderate overall family environment are found exhibit higher school performance in comparison to those experiencing coming for low overall family environment.

Since the mean school performance scores of children belonging to enriched overall family environment group is higher than that of both moderate and low overall family environment group. It can be said that children experiencing Enriched Overall Family Environment are found to have higher School Performance in comparison to children belonging to Moderate Overall Family Environment and Low Family Environment. Also children experiencing Moderate Overall Family Environment are found to have higher School Performance in comparison children experiencing Low Overall Family Environment (as perceived by Children).

Table 4.8

Significance of Difference in Mean School Performance Scores of Elementary School Children at Different Level of Family Environment on *Achievement Orientation* (As Perceived by Children)

Groups	*N*	*M*	*S.D*	*t-ratio*	*Level of significance*
Enriched family environment	91	83.703	14.629		
Vs				5.3069	0.01
Low family environment	55	69.982	15.438		
Enriched Achievement orientation	91	83.703	14.629		

Contd.

Contd.

Groups	*N*	*M*	*S.D*	*t-ratio*	*Level of significance*
Vs				2.2748	0.05
Moderate Achievement orientation	39	76.615	16.938		
Moderate Achievement orientation	39	76.615			
Vs				1.9402	0.05
Low Achievement orientation	55	69.982	15.438		

Table 4.8 shows that the mean school performance scores of enriched achievement orientation group is 83.703 and that of low achievement orientation group is 69.982 with SDs 14.629 and 15.438 respectively. The obtained 't' value is 5.3069 and this is found to be significant at 0.01 level. Thus, it can be inferred that the two groups differ significantly in their school performance. The mean school performance score of enriched achievement orientation is higher than that of low achievement orientation group. It indicates that children experiencing enriched achievement orientation are found to have higher school performance than those experiencing low achievement orientation.

Table 4.8 further shows that the mean school performance score of enriched achievement orientation group is 83.703 and that of moderate achievement orientation group is 76.615 , with SDs 14.629 and 16.939 respectively. The obtained 't'-value is 2.748 and this is found to be significant at 0.05 level of significance. It implies that the two groups differ significantly in their school performance. The mean school performance score of enriched achievement orientation is higher than the moderate achievement orientation group. It suggests that children with enriched achievement orientation are found to have higher school performance in comparison to those coming from moderate achievement orientation group.

It can also be seen in Table 4.8 that mean school performance score of moderate achievement orientation group is 76.615 and that of low achievement orientation group is 69.982, with SDs 16.938 and 15.438 respectively. The obtained 't' value for these two groups is 1.9402, and this is found to be significant at 0.05 level of significance. It means that the two groups differ significantly in their school performance. The mean school performance of moderate achievement orientation is higher than that of low achievement orientation. It indicates that children experiencing moderate achievement orientation exhibit higher school performance in comparison to those experiencing low achievement orientation.

Since the mean school performance score of children belonging to enriched family environment group is higher than that of both moderate and low family environment group and that of moderate group is higher than that of low family environment group, it can be said that children experiencing Enriched Achievement Orientation are found to exhibit higher School Performance in comparison to children experiencing to Moderate Achievement Orientation and Low Achievement Orientation. Further it can also be inferred that Moderate Achievement Orientation group of children exhibit higher school performance than Low Achievement Orientation group of children.

Table 4.9
Significance of Difference in Mean School Performance Scores of Elementary Schoool Children at Different Level of Family Environment on *Cognitive Stimulation* (As Perceived by Children)

Groups	*N*	*M*	*S.D*	*t-ratio*	*Level of significance*
Enriched Cognitive stimulation	68	85.309	14.702		
Vs				5.6384	0.01
Low Cognitive stimulation	47	69.234	15.251		
Enriched Cognitive stimulation	68	85.309	14.702		
Vs				3.1526	0.01
Moderate Cognitive stimulation	70	77.129	15.773		
Moderate Cognitive stimulation	70	77.129	15.773		
Vs				2.7073	0.01
Low Cognitive stimulation	47	69.234	15.251		

Table 4.9 shows that the mean school performance scores of enriched cognitive stimulation group, is 85.309 and that of low cognitive stimulation group is 69.234, with SDs 14.702 and 15.251 respectively. The obtained 't' value is 5.6384 and this is found to be significant at 0.01 level. Thus it can be inferred that the two groups differ significantly in their school performance. The mean school performance score of enriched cognitive stimulation group is higher than that of low cognitive stimulation group. The scores indicate that children experiencing enriched cognitive stimulation are found to have higher school performance than those experiencing low cognitive stimulation.

Table 4.9 further shows that mean school performance score of enriched cognitive stimulation group is 85.309 and that of moderate cognitive stimulation group is 77.129, with SDs 14.702 and 15.773 respectively. The obtained 't'value is 3.1526 and it is found to be significant at 0.01 level. It implies that the two groups differ significantly in their school performance. The mean school performance score of enriched cognitive stimulation is higher than that of moderate cognitive stimulation group. It suggests that children experiencing enriched cognitive stimulation are found to have higher school performance in comparison to those coming from moderate cognitive stimulation.

It can also be seen in Table 4.9 that mean school performance score of moderate cognitive stimulation group is 77.129 and that of low cognitive stimulation group is 69.234, with SDs 15.773 and 15.251 respectively. The obtained 't' value for these two groups is 2.7073, and this is found to be significant at 0.05 level of significance. It means that the two groups differ significantly in their school performance. The mean school performance score of moderate cognitive stimulation group is higher than that of low cognitive stimulation group. It indicates that children experiencing moderate cognitive stimulation are found to have higher school performance than those experiencing low cognitive stimulation.

Since the mean school performance score of children belonging to enriched cognitive stimulation group is higher than that of both moderate and low cognitive stimulation group and that of moderate group is higher than that of low cognitive stimulation group. It can be said that children experiencing Enriched Cognitive Stimulation are found to have superior school performance in comparison to children experiencing Moderate Cognitive Stimulation and Low Cognitive Stimulation. Also Moderate Cognitive Stimulation group of children exhibit higher school performance in comparison to Low Cognitive Stimulation group of children, *as perceived by children.*

Table 4.10

Significance of Difference in Mean School Performance Scores of Elementary School Children at Different Level of Family Environment on *Recreational Orientation* (As Perceived by Children)

Groups	*N*	*M*	*S.D*	*t-ratio*	*Level of significance*
Enriched Recreational orientation	70	85.986	13.691		
Vs				5.8361	0.01
Low Recreational orientation	54	70.519	15.320		
Enriched Recreational orientation	70	85.986	13.691		
Vs				3.7797	0.01
Moderate Recreational orientation	61	75.852	16.586		
Moderate Recreational orientation	61	75.852	16.586		
Vs				1.7924	0.05
Low Recreational orientation	54	70.519	15.320		

Table 4.10 indicates that the mean school performance scores of enriched recreational orientation group, is 85.986 and that of low recreational orientation group is 70.519, with SDs 13.691 and 15.320 respectively. The obtained 't' value is 5.8361 and this is found to be significant at 0.01 level. It suggests that the two groups differ significantly in their school performance. Mean school performance score of enriched recreational orientation is higher than that of low recreational orientation group. The scores indicate that children experiencing enriched recreational orientation are found to have higher school performance than those experiencing to low recreational orientation.

It can also be observed from Table 4.10 that mean school performance score of enriched recreational orientation group is 85.986 and that of moderate recreational orientation group is 75.852, with SDs 13.691 and 16.586 respectively. The obtained 't' value is 3.7797 and it is found to be significant at 0.o1 level of significance. It implies that the two groups differ significantly in their school performance. Higher mean school performance score of enriched recreational orientation group than moderate recreational orientation group suggest that children experiencing enriched recreational orientation are found to have higher school performance in comparison to those experiencing moderate recreational orientation.

It can also be seen in Table 4.10 that mean school performance score of moderate recreational orientation group is 75.852 and that of low group is 70.519, with SDs 16.586 and 15.320 respectively. The obtained 't' value for these two groups is 1.7924, and this is found to be significant at .05 level of significance. It means that the two groups differ significantly in their school performance. Higher mean school performance score of moderate recreational orientation group than low recreational orientation group suggest that children experiencing moderate recreational orientation are found to have higher school performance in comparison to those experiencing low recreational orientation.

Since the mean school performance score of children belonging to enriched recreational orientation group is higher than that of both moderate and low recreational orientation group and that of moderate group is higher than that of low recreational orientation group. It can be said that children experiencing Enriched Recreational Orientation are found to have superior school performance in comparison to children experiencing Moderate recreational orientation and Low recreational orientation. In addition to this it can also be said that Moderate Recreational Orientation group of children exhibit higher school performance in comparison to Low Recreational Orientation group of children, *as perceived by children.*

Table 4.11 below shows that the mean school performance scores of enriched Home structure group, is 85.844 and that of low home structure group is 69.431 with SDs 13.672 and 14.128 respectively. The obtained 't' value is 6.7750 and this is found to be significant at 0.01 level. Thus it can be inferred that the two groups differ significantly in their school performance. Mean school performance score of enriched home structure group is higher than that of low home structure group. The scores suggest that children experiencing enriched home structure group are found to have higher school performance than those experiencing low Home structure.

Table 4.11 further shows that mean school performance score of enriched home structure group is 85.844 and that of moderate home structure group is 76.340, with SDs 13.672 and 17.458 respectively. The obtained 't'value is 3.2554 and it is found to be significant at 0.01 level. It implies that the two groups differ significantly in their school performance. Mean school performance score of enriched home structure group is higher than that of moderate home structure group. It suggests that children experiencing enriched home structure are found to have better school performance in comparison to those experiencing moderate home structure.

Table 4.11

Significance of Difference in Mean School Performance Scores of Elementary School Children at Different Level of Family Environment on *Home Structure* (As Perceived by Children)

Groups	*N*	*M*	*S.D*	*t-ratio*	*Level of significance*
Enriched Home structure	77	85.844	13.672		
Vs				6.7750	0.01
Low Home structure	58	69.431	14.128		
Enriched Home structure	77	85.844	13.672		
Vs				3.2554	0.01
Moderate Home structure	50	76.340	17.458		
Moderate Home structure	50	76.340	17.458		
Vs				2.2372	0.05
Low Home structure	58	69.431	14.128		

It can also be seen in Table 4.11 that mean school performance score of moderate home structure group is 76.340 and that of low home structure group is 69.431, with SDs 17.458 and 14.128 respectively. The obtained 't' value for these two groups is 2.2372, and this is found to be significant at 0.05 level. It means that the two groups differ significantly in their school performance. Mean school performance score of moderate home structure group is higher than that of low home structure group .It suggests that children experiencing moderate home structure are found to have higher school performance in comparison to those experiencing low home structure in the family.

Since the mean school performance score of children belonging to enriched family environment group is higher than that of both moderate and low family environment group and that of moderate group is higher than that of low home structure group, it can be said that children experiencing Enriched Home Structure are found to have higher school performance in comparison to children experiencing Moderate Home Structure in the family and those belonging to Moderate Home Structure group exhibit higher school performance in comparison Low Home Structure group of children, *as perceived by children.*

Table 4.12 below shows that the mean school performance score of enriched Language stimulation group, is 87.177and that of low language stimulation group is 68.653, with SDs 12.266 and 14.815 respectively. The obtained 't' value is 8.4279 and this is found to be significant at .01 level. Thus it can be inferred that the two groups differ significantly in their school performance. Mean school performance score of Enriched language stimulation is higher than that of Low language stimulation group. The scores indicate that children experiencing enriched language stimulation are found to have higher school performance than those experiencing to low language stimulation in the family.

Table 4.12

Significance of Difference in Mean School Performance of Elementary School Children at Different Level of familyEnvironment on *Language Stimulation* (As Perceived by Children)

Groups	*N*	*M*	*S.D*	*t-ratio*	*Level of significance*
Enriched Language stimulation	79	87.177	12.266		
Vs				8.4279	.01
Low Language stimulation	75	68.653	14.815		
Enriched Language stimulation	79	87.177	12.266		
Vs				2.7604	.01
Moderate Language stimulation	31	78.000	16.841		
Moderate Language stimulation	31	78.000	16.841		
Vs				2.6897	.01
Low Language stimulation	75	68.653	14.815		

Table 4.12 further shows that mean school performance score of enriched language stimulation group is 87.177 and that of moderate Language stimulation group is 78.000, with SDs 12.266 and 16.841 respectively. The obtained 't'value is 2.7604 and this is found to be significant at .01 level. It implies that the two groups differ significantly in their school performance. Mean school performance score of enriched language stimulation is higher than that of moderate language stimulation group. The scores indicate that children experiencing enriched language stimulation are found to exhibit higher school performance than those experiencing moderate language stimulation.

Table 4.12 also shows that mean school performance score of moderate language stimulation group is 78.000 and that of low language stimulation group is 68.653, with SDs 16.841 and 14.815 respectively. The obtained 't' value for these two groups is 2.6897, and this is found to be significant at .01 level. It means that the two groups differ significantly in their school performance. Mean school performance score of moderate language stimulation is higher than that of low language stimulation group. The scores indicate that children experiencing moderate language stimulation are found to have higher school performance in comparison to those experiencing low language stimulation.

Since the mean school performance scores of children belonging to enriched language stimulation group is higher than that of both moderate and low Language stimulation group and that of moderate group is higher than that of low language stimulation group, it can be said that children experiencing Enriched Language Stimulation are found to exhibit higher school performance in comparison to children experiencing Moderate Language Stimulation and Low Language stimulation and those belonging to Moderate group exhibit higher school performance than Low Language stimulation group of children *as perceived by children.*

For a clear comprehension of results comparisons of 't', ratios and means school performance score of table 4.8 to 4.12 are presented in table 4.13 and 4.14 respectively.

It can be observed from table 4.13 that significant differences in mean school performance score of elementary school children at different level of family environment *as perceived by Children* are found at all the three level family environment i.e., Enriched - Low: Enriched – Moderate: and Moderate – Low level family environment with respect to overall family environment and all the five dimensions of family environment.

Results presented in tables 4.14 and reveal that children experiencing Enriched Family Environment exhibit higher school performance than those experiencing either Moderate or Low Family Environment with respect to Overall Family Environment and its five dimensions. It is also observed that children experiencing Moderate Family

Table 4.13

Comparison of 't' Ratios Obtained for School Performance Different Level of their Family Environment with Respect to Overall Family Environment and its Five Dimension (As Perceived by Children)

Variables → FE ↓ groups	*OFE*	*AO*	*LS*	*RO*	*HS*	*LS*
En vs Lo	9.3967**	5.3069 **	5.6384**	5.8361**	6.7750**	8.4279**
En vs Mo	5.5905**	2.2748*	3.1526**	3.7797**	3.2554**	2.7604**
Mo vs Lo	1.9636*	1.9402*	2.7073**	1.7924*	2.2372*	2.6897**

Table 4.14

Comparison of Mean School Performance Scores of Elementary School Children at Different Level of their Family Environment (As Perceived by Children)

Variables → FE ↓ groups	*OFE*	*AO*	*LS*	*RO*	*HS*	*LS*
Enriched	89.261	83.703	85.309	85.986	85.844	87.177
Moderate	74.564	76.615	77.129	75.852	76.340	78.000
Low	68.574	69.982	69.234	70.519	69.431	68.653

** Significant at 0.01 level; *Significant at 0.05 level
OFE = Overall family environment, AO = Achievement Orientation,
CS = Cognitive Stimulation, RO = Recreated Orientation,
HS = Home Structure, LS = Language Stimulation,
F.E. = Family Environment, En = Enriched, Mo = Moderate, Lo = Low.

Environment exhibit higher school performance than those experiencing

Low Family Environment with respect to Overall Family Environment and its five dimensions viz. Achievement Orientation, Cognitive Stimulation, Recreational Orientation, Home Structure and Language stimulation *as perceived by Children*. Thus on the basis of results it can be concluded that better the Family Environment higher is the School Performance.

Therefore Hy 5 of the present study that 'If a child experiences better family environment (school – focussed parent child interactions) then the child will exhibit higher school performance than the one, who experiences not so good family environment (as perceived by Children)' is retained for Overall Family Environment its five dimensions viz. Achievement Orientation, Cognitive Stimulation, Recreational Orientation, Home Structure and Language stimulation (*as perceived by Children)* at all the three levels of family environment i.e. Enriched – Low, Enriched – Moderate and Moderate – Low.

School Performance Differentials of Elementary School Children at Different Levels of Family Environment as Perceived by *Parents*

School performance differentials of elementary school children at different levels of family environment and its five dimensions *as perceived by Parents* are presented below in tables 4.15 to 4.20.

Table 4.15

Significance of Difference in Mean School Performance Scores of Elementary School Children at Different Levels of Overall Family Environment (As Perceived by Parents)

Groups	*N*	*M*	*S.D*	*t-ratio*	*Level of Significance*
Enriched Overall Family environment	64	87.406	10.834		
Vs				8.4931	0.01
Low Overall family environment	50	66.280	14.754		
Enriched Overall Family environment	64	87.406	10.834		
Vs				3.6456	0.01
Moderate Overall Family environment	61	78.311	16.364		
Moderate Overall Family environment	61	78.311	16.364		
Vs				4.0689	0.01
Low Overall Family environment	50	66.280	14.754		

Table 4.15 shows that the mean school performance score of enriched overall family environment group, is 87.406 and that of low overall family environment group is 66.280 , with SDs 10.834 and 14.754 respectively. The obtained 't' value is 8.4931 and this is found to be significant at 0.01 level. Thus it can be inferred that the two groups differ significantly in their school performance. It can also be seen that mean school performance score of enriched overall family environment is higher than low overall family environment group. The scores indicate that children experiencing enriched overall family environment are found to have higher school performance than those experiencing low overall family environment.

Table 4.15 further shows that mean school performance score of enriched overall family environment group is 87.406 and that of moderate overall family environment group is 78.311, with SDs 10.834 and 16.364 respectively. The obtained 't'value is found to be significant at 0.01 level. It implies that the two groups differ significantly in their school performance. Above table also reveals that mean school performance score of enriched family environment is higher than that of moderate overall family environment group. It suggests that children experiencing enriched overall family environment are found to have better school performance in comparison to those experiencing moderate overall family environment.

It can also be seen in Table 4.15 that mean school performance score of moderate overall family environment group is 78.311 and that of low overall family environment group is 66.280 , with SDs 16.364 and 14.754 respectively. The obtained 't' value for these two groups is 4.0689, and this is found to be significant at 0.01 level. It means that the two groups differ significantly in their school performance. Mean school performance score of moderate overall family environment group is higher than that of low overall family environment group. The results indicate that children experiencing moderate overall family environment are found to have higher better school performance than those experiencing low overall family environment .

Since the mean school performance scores of children belonging to enriched overall family environment group is higher than that of both moderate and low overall family environment group and that of moderate group is higher than that of low family environment group, it can be said that children experiencing Enriched Overall Family environment are found to exhibit higher school performance in comparison to children experiencing Moderate Overall Family Environment and Low Overall Family Environment. In addition to this it can also be said that children experiencing Moderate Overall Family environment are found to exhibit higher School Performance in comparison to those experiencing Low Overall Family Environment *as perceived by parents.*

Table 4.16
Significance of Difference in Mean School Performance Scores of Elementary School Children at Different Level of Family Environment on *Achievement Orientation* (As Perceived by Parents)

Groups	*N*	*M*	*S.D*	*t-ratio*	*Level of significance*
Enriched Achievement orientation	76	86.368	12.204		
Vs				6.4484	0.01
Low Achievement orientation	50	69.320	15.859		
Enriched Achievement orientation	76	86.368	12.204		
Vs				4.2519	0.01
Moderate Achievement orientation	49	74.592	16.729		
Moderate Achievement orientation	49	74.592	16.729		
Vs				1.6085	NS
Low Achievement orientation.	50	69.320	15.859		

Table 4.16 shows that the mean School performance scores of enriched achievement orientation group, is 86.368 and that of low achievement orientation group is 69.320 with SDs 12.204 and 15.859 respectively. The obtained 't' value is 6.4484 and this is found to be significant at 0.01 level. Thus it can be inferred that the two groups differ significantly in their school performance. The above table also shows that mean school performance score of enriched achievement orientation group is higher than low achievement orientation group. The scores indicate that children experiencing enriched achievement orientation are found to have higher school performance than those experiencing low achievement orientation.

Table 4.16 further shows that mean school performance score of enriched achievement orientation group is 86.368 and that of moderate achievement orientation group is 74.592, with SDs 12.204 and 16.729

respectively. The obtained 't'value is 4.2519 and it is found to be significant at 0.01 level. It implies that the two groups differ significantly in their school performance. Mean school performance score of enriched family environment is higher than moderate family environment group. It suggests that children experiencing enriched family environment are found to have higher school performance in comparison to those experiencing moderate achievement orientation group.

It can also be seen in Table 4.16 that mean school performance score of moderate achievement orientation group is 74.592 and that of low achievement orientation group is 69.320, with SDs 16.729 and 15.859 respectively. The obtained 't' value for these two groups is 1.6085, and this is not found to be significant even at 0.05 level. It means that the two groups do not differ significantly in their school performance.

Since the mean school performance scores of children belonging to enriched achievement orientation group is higher than that of both moderate and low family environment group, it can be said that children experiencing Enriched Achievement Orientation are found to have higher School Performance in comparison to children experiencing Moderate Achievement Orientation and Low Achievement Orientation *as perceived by parents.*

Table 4.17 shows that the mean School performance scores of enriched cognitive stimulation group, is 85.288 and that of low cognitive stimulation group is 68.333, with SDs 12.787 and 16.259 respectively. The obtained 't' value is 6.4647 and this is found to be significant at 0.01 level. Thus it can be inferred that the two groups differ significantly in their school performance. The mean school performance score of enriched cognitive stimulation group is higher than that of low cognitive stimulation group. The scores indicate that children experiencing enriched cognitive stimulation are found to have higher school performance than those experiencing low cognitive stimulation.

Table 4.17 further shows that mean school performance score of enriched cognitive stimulation group is 85.288 and that of moderate cognitive stimulation group is 79.200, with SDs 12.787and 15.630 respectively. The obtained 't'value is 2.1983 and it is found to be significant at 0.05 level. It implies that the two groups differ significantly in their school performance. The mean school performance score of enriched cognitive stimulation group of children is higher than that of moderate cognitive stimulation group. It suggests that children experiencing enriched cognitive stimulation are found to have higher better school performance in comparison to those coming from Moderate Cognitive stimulation .

Table 4.17
Significance of Difference in Mean School Performance Scores of Elementary School Children at Different Levels of Family Environment on *Cognitive Stimulation* (As Perceived by Parents)

Groups	*N*	*M*	*S.D*	*t-ratio*	*Level of significance*
Enriched Cognitive stimulation	73	85.288	12.787		
Vs				6.4647	0.01
Low Cognitive stimulation	57	68.333	16.259		
Enriched Cognitive stimulation	73	85.288	12.787		
Vs				2.1983	0.05
Moderate Cognitive stimulation	45	79.200	15.630		
Moderate Cognitive stimulation	45	79.200	15.630		
Vs				3.4249	0.01
Low Cognitive stimulation	57	68.333	16.259		

It can also be seen in Table 4.17 that mean school performance score of moderate cognitive stimulation group is 79.200 and that of low cognitive stimulation group is 68.333, with SDs 15.630 and 16.259 respectively. The obtained 't' value for these two groups is 3.4249, and this is found to be significant at 0.01 level. It means that the two groups differ significantly in their school performance. The mean school performance score of moderate cognitive stimulation group is higher than that of low cognitive stimulation group. It indicates that children experiencing moderate cognitive stimulation are found to exhibit higher school performance than those experiencing low cognitive stimulation.

Since the mean school performance scores of children belonging to enriched cognitive stimulation group is higher than that of both moderate and low cognitive stimulation group and that of moderate group is higher than that of low cognitive stimulation group. It can be said that children experiencing Enriched Cognitive Stimulation are found to exhibit superior school performance in comparison to children experiencncing Moderate Cognitive Stimulation and Low Cognitive Stimulation. Also

Moderate Cognitive Stimulation group of children exhibit higher school performance in comparison to Low Cognitive Stimulation group of children, *as perceived by parents.*

Table 4.18

Significance of Difference in Mean School Performance Scores of Elementary School Children at Different Levels of Family Environment on *Recreational Orientation* (As Perceived by Parents)

Groups	*N*	*M*	*S.D*	*t-ratio*	*Level of significance*
Enriched Recreational orientation	70	84.842	12.847		
Vs				4.8910	0.01
Low Recreational orientation	43	70.279	16.729		
Enriched Recreational orientation	70	84.843	12.847		
Vs				3.2819	0.01
Moderate Recreational orientation	62	76.194	16.866		
Moderate Recreational orientation	62	76.194	16.866		
Vs				1.7755	0.05
Low Recreational orientation	43	70.279	16.729		

Table 4.18 indicates that the mean School performance scores of enriched recreational orientation group, is 84.843 and that of low recreational orientation group is 70.279, with SDs 12.847 and 16.729 respectively. The obtained 't' value is 4.8910 and this is found to be significant at .01 level. It suggests that the two groups differ significantly in their school performance. Mean school performance score of enriched recreational orientation is higher than that of low recreational orientation group. The scores indicate that children experiencing enriched recreational orientation are found to exhibit superior school performance than those experiencing low recreational orientation.

It can also be observed from Table 4.18 that mean school performance score of enriched Recreational orientation group is 84.843 and that of moderate recreational orientation group is 76.194, with SDs 12.847 and

16.866 respectively. The obtained 't'value is 3.2819 and it is found to be significant at 0.01 level. It implies that the two groups differ significantly in their school performance. Higher mean school performance score of enriched recreational orientation group than moderate recreational orientation group suggest that children experiencing enriched recreational orientation are found to exhibit have higher school performance in comparison to those experiencing moderate recreational orientation.

It can also be seen in Table 4.18 that mean school performance score of moderate recreational orientation group is 76.194 and that of low group is 70.279, with SDs 16.866 and 16.279 respectively. The obtained 't' value for these two groups is 1.7755, and this is found to be significant at 0.05 level. It means that the two groups differ significantly in their school performance. Higher mean school performance score of moderate recreational orientation group than low recreational orientation group suggest that children experiencing moderate recreational orientation are found to have higher school performance in comparison to those experiencing low recreational orientation.

Since the mean school performance scores of children belonging to enriched recreational orientation group is higher than that of both moderate and low recreational orientation group and that of moderate group is higher than that of low recreational orientation group, it can be said that children experiencing Enriched Recreational Orientation are found to exhibit higher school performance in comparison to children experiencing Moderate recreational orientation and Low recreational orientation. In addition to this it can also be said that Moderate Recreational Orientation group of children exhibit higher school performance in comparison to Low Recreational Orientation group of children, *as perceived by parents.*

Table 4.19 shows that the mean School performance scores of enriched Home structure group, is 84.533 and that of low home structure group is 69.160 with SDs 14.292 and 15.160 respectively. The obtained 't' value is 5.8879 and this is found to be significant at 0.01 level. The scores suggest that the two groups differ significantly in their school performance. Mean school performance score of enriched home structure group is higher than that of low home structure group. The scores indicate that children experiencing enriched home structure are found to exhibit higher school performance than those experiencing low home structure.

Table 4.19
Significance of Difference in Mean School Performance Scores of Elementary School Children at Different Level of Family Environment on *Home Structure* (As Perceived by Parents)

Groups	*N*	*M*	*S.D*	*t-ratio*	*Level of significance*
Enriched Home structure	92	84.533	14.292		
Vs				5.8879	0.01
Low Home structure	50	69.160	15.160		
Enriched Home structure	92	84.533	14.292		
Vs				3.2228	0.01
Moderate Home structure	33	74.242	16.222		
Moderate Home structure	33	74.242	16.222		
Vs				1.4335	NS
Low Home structure	50	69.160	15.160		

Table 4.19 further shows that mean school performance score of enriched home structure group is 84.533 and that of moderate home structure group is 74.242, with SDs 14.292 and 16.222 respectively. The obtained 't' value is 3.2228 and it is found to be significant at 0.01 level. It implies that the two groups differ significantly in their school performance. Mean school performance score of enriched home structure group is higher than that of moderate home structure group. It suggests that children experiencing enriched Home structure are found to exhibit better school performance in comparison to those experiencing moderate home structure.

It can also be seen in Table 4.19 that mean school performance score of moderate home structure group is 74.242 and that of low home structure group is 69.160, with SDs 16.222 and 15.160 respectively. The obtained 't' value for these two groups is 1.4335, and this is not found to be significant even at 0.05 level. It means that the two groups don't differ significantly in their school performance.

Since the mean school performance scores of children belonging to enriched family environment group is higher than that of both moderate and low family environment group, it can be said that children experiencing Enriched Home Structure are found to exhibit higher School Performance in comparison to children experiencing Moderate Home Structure and Low Home Structure *as perceived by parents.*

Table 4.20
Significance of Difference in Mean School Performance Scores of Elementary School Children at Different Level of Family Environment on *Language Stimulation* (As Perceived by Parents)

Groups	*N*	*M*	*S.D*	*t-ratio*	*Level of significance*
Enriched Language stimulation	61	84.066	13.581		
Vs				3.9299	0.05
Low Language stimulation	64	73.078	17.515		
Enriched Language stimulation	61	84.066	13.581		
Vs				2.2780	0.01
Moderate Language stimulation	50	77.600	15.862		
Moderate Language stimulation	50	77.600	15.862		
Vs				1.4426	NS
Low Language stimulation	64	73.078	17.515		

Table 4.20 shows that the mean school performance score of enriched language stimulation group, is 84.066 and that of low language stimulation group is 73.078, with SDs 13.581 and 17.515 respectively. The obtained 't' value is 3.9299 and this is found to be significant at 0.05 level of significance. Thus it can be inferred that the two groups differ significantly in their school performance. Mean school performance score of enriched language stimulation group is higher than that of low language stimulation group. The scores indicate that children experiencing enriched language stimulation are found to have higher school performance than those experiencing low language stimulation.

Table 4.20 further shows that mean school performance score of enriched language stimulation group is 84.066 and that of moderate language stimulation group is 77.600, with SDs 13.581 and 15.862 respectively. The obtained 't'value is 2.2780 found to be significant at 0.01 level. It implies that the two groups differ significantly in their school performance. Mean school performance score of enriched language stimulation group is higher than that of moderate language stimulation group. The scores indicate that children experiencing enriched language stimulation are found to exhibit higher school performance than those experiencing moderate language stimulation.

Table 4.20 that mean school performance score of moderate Language stimulation group is 77.600 and that of low Language stimulation group is 73.078, with SDs 15.862 and 17.515 respectively. The obtained 't' value for these two groups is 1.4426, and this is not found to be significant even at .05 level. It means that the two groups do not differ significantly in their school performance.

Since the mean school performance score of children belonging to enriched language stimulation group is higher than that of both moderate and low language stimulation group, it can be said that children experiencing Enriched Language Stimulation are found to exhibit higher School Performance in comparison to those experiencing Moderate Language Stimulation and Low Language Stimulation *as perceived by parents.*

For clear comprehension of results comparison of 't'. ratios and means school performance scores of table 4.15 to 4.20 are presented in table 4.21 and 4.22.

Table 4.21

Comparison of 't' Ratios Obtained for School Performance Differentials of Elementary School Children at Different Level of their Family Environment with Respect to Overall Family Environment and its Five Dimension (As Perceived by Parents)

Variables →	*OFE*	*AO*	*LS*	*RO*	*HS*	*LS*
FE ↓ groups						
En vs Lo	8.493**	6.4484**	6.4647**	4.8910**	5.8879**	3.9299**
En vs Mo	3.6456**	4.2519**	2.1983**	3.2819**	3.2228**	2.2780*
Mo vs Lo	4.0689**	1.6085	3.4249**	1.7755*	1.4335	1.4426

** Significant at .01 level; * Significant at 0.05 level

OFE = Overall family environment, AO = Achievement Orientation, CS = Cognitive Stimulation, RO = Recreated Orientation, HS = Home Structure, LS = Language Stimulation, F.E. = Family Environment, En = Enriched, Mo = Moderate, Lo = Low.

Table 4.22
Comparison of Mean School Performance Scores of Elementary School Children at Different Level of their Family Environment (As Perceived by Parents)

Variables → *FE* ↓ *groups*	*OFE*	*AO*	*CS*	*RO*	*HS*	*LS*
Enriched	87.406	86.368	85.288	84.842	84.533	84.066
Moderate	78.311	74.592	79.200	76.194	74.242	77.600
Low	66.280	69.320	68.333	70.279	69.160	73.078

It can be observed from table 4.21 that significant differences in the mean school performance of elementary school children at different levels of family environment as perceived by parents are found for Enriched – Low family environment and Enriched – Moderate family environment with respect to overall family environment and all the file dimensions of family environment. Such differences are also observer for Moderate – Low family environment with respect to overall family environment, Cognitive stimulation and Recreational orientation.

Results presented in table 4.22 reveals that children experiencing enriched family environment exhibit higher school performance than those experiencing either moderate family environment or low family environment with respect to Overall family environment all the five dimension viz. Achievement orientation, Cognitive stimulation Recreational orientation, Home structure and Language stimulation. Scores also reveals that children experiencing moderate family environment exhibit higher school performance than those experiencing low family environment with respect to all the five dimension of family environment as perceived by Parents.

Therefore Hy 6 of the present study that ' If a child experiences better family environment (school – focussed parent child interactions) then the child will exhibit higher school performance than the one, who experiences not so good family environment (as perceived by Parents)' is retained at Enriched - Low level and Enriched – Moderate level for Overall Family Environment its five dimensions viz. Achievement Orientation, Cognitive Stimulation, Recreational Orientation, Home Structure and Language stimulation: at Moderate – Low level for Overall family environment, Cognitive stimulation and Recreational orientation. (*as perceived by Parents*).

Impact of Family Environment on the School Performance of Elementary School Children belonging to Similar Intelligence Group

In this section an attempt has been made to study the impact of family environment (as perceived by children and parents) on the school performance of elementary school children belonging to *similar intelligence group.* For this purpose subjects were classified into three groups i.e. high intelligence; middle intelligence and low intelligence groups, by adopting the criterion of Mean ± ½ SD. Classification of subjects, on the basis of similar intelligence has been done to isolate the influence of intelligence on their school performance. Classification of subjects into three groups, on the basis of their score value on intelligence test, is presented below in Table-4.17.

Table 4.23

Classification of Subjects into Three Groups in Terms of their Intelligence Scores

Variable	Mean	SD	Upper Intelligence	Moderate Intelligence	Low Intelligence
Intelligence	27.41	7.82	31 and above	Between 31 and 24	24 and below

In section 4.3.1 the school performance differentials of elementary school children belonging to similar intelligence group are examined at different levels of overall family environment *as perceived by children.*

For a clear and precise comprehension school performance differentials are also examined at different levels of all the five dimensions of family environment *as perceived by Children* in section 4.3.2.

A similar procedure will be followed for examining school performance differentials of elementary school children belonging to similar intelligence groups at different levels of overall family environment as well as its five dimensions *as perceived by parents.*

School performance Differentials in Elementary School Children belonging to Similar intelligence group at different levels of *Overall Family Environment* (as perceived by children)

School performance differentials in elementary school children belonging to three groups of similar intelligence viz. high; middle and low intelligence group, at different levels of Overall Family environment *as perceived by children* are presented in Tables 4.24 – 4.26.

Table 4.24 shows that the mean school performance score of enriched family environment group, is 92.371 and that of low family environment

Table 4.24

Significance of Difference in Mean School Performance Scores of Elementary School Children Belonging to High Intelligence Group at Different Levels of *Overall Family Environment* (As Perceived by Children)

Groups	*N*	*M*	*S.D*	*t-ratio*	*Level of significance*
Enriched Overall Family Environment	35	92.371	6.871		
Vs				3.6839	.01
Low Overall Family Environment	18	76.071	15.975		
Enriched Overall Family Environment	35	92.371	6.871		
Vs				2.9878	.01
Moderate Overall Family Environment	14	79.833	17.108		
Moderate Overall Family Environment	18	79.833	17.108		
Vs				.6406	NS
Low Overall Family Environment	14	76.071	15.975		

group is 76.071, with SDs 6.871 and 15.975 respectively. The obtained 't' value is 3.6839 and this is found to be significant at 0.01 level. Thus it can be inferred that the two groups differ significantly in their school performance. The mean school performance score of enriched family environment group of children belonging to high intelligence group is higher than that of low family environment group. The scores indicate that high intelligence group of children experiencing enriched family environment are found to exhibit higher school performance than those experiencing low family environment.

Table 4.24 further shows that mean school performance score of enriched family environment group is 92.371 and that of moderate family environment group is 79.833, with SDs 6.871 and 17.108 respectively. The obtained 't'value is 2.9878, and this is found to be significant at 0.01 level. It implies that the two groups differ significantly in their school performance. Mean school performance score of enriched family environment is higher than that of moderate family environment group. The scores indicate that children of high intelligence group experiencing enriched family environment are found to exhibit higher school performance than those experiencing moderate family environment.

Table 4.24 indicates that mean school performance score of moderate family environment group is 79.833 and that of low family environment group is 76.071, with SDs 17.108 and 15.975 respectively. The obtained 't' value for these two groups is 0.6406, which is less than the table value and this is found to be not significant even at 0.05 level. It means that the two groups do not differ significantly in their school performance.

Since the mean school performance score of children of high intelligence group experiencing enriched family environment is higher than those experiencing either moderate or low family environment, it can be said that children belonging to *high intelligence group* and experiencing Enriched Overall Family Environment are found to have superior School Performance in comparison to children experiencing Moderate Family Environment or Low family environment.

Table 4.25

Significance of Difference in Mean School Performance Scores of Elementary School Children Belonging to Moderate Intelligence Group at Different Levels of *[Overall Family Environment]* (As Perceived by Children)

Groups	*N*	*M*	*S.D*	*t-ratio*	*Level of significance*
Enriched Overall Family Environment	15	89.933	8.925		
Vs				3.7998	0.01
Low Overall Family Environment	13	70.154	18.905		
Enriched Overall Family Environment	15	89.933	8.925		
Vs				3.0659	0.01
Moderate Overall Family Environment	16	73.813	16.829		
Moderate Overall Family Environment	16	73.813	18.905		
Vs				0.5508	NS
Low Overall Family Environment	13	70.154	16.829		

Table 4.25 shows that the mean School performance scores of enriched family environment group, is 89.933 and that of low family

environment group is 70.154, with SDs 8.925 and 16.829 respectively. The obtained 't' value is 3.7998 and this is found to be significant at 0.01 level. Thus it can be inferred that the two groups differ significantly in their school performance. Mean school performance score of enriched family environment is higher than that of low family environment group. The scores indicate that children of moderate intelligence group experiencing enriched overall family environment are found to exhibit higher school performance than those experiencing Low family environment.

Table 4.25 further shows that mean school performance score of enriched family environment group is 89.933 and that of moderate family environment group is 73.813, with SDs 8.925 and 18.905 respectively. The obtained 't'value is 3.0659 and this is found to be significant at 0.01 level. It implies that the two groups differ significantly in their school performance. Mean school performance score of enriched family environment is higher than that of moderate family environment group. The scores indicate that children of moderate intelligence group experiencing enriched overall family environment are found to exhibit higher school performance than those experiencing moderate family environment.

Table 4.25 shows that mean school performance score of moderate family environment group is 73.813 and that of low family environment group is 70.154, with SDs 18.905, and 16.829 respectively. The obtained 't' value for these two groups is 0.5508, which is less than the table value and this is found to be not significant even at 0.05 level. It means that the two groups do not differ significantly in their school performance.

Since the mean school performance score of children of moderate intelligence group experiencing enriched family environment group is higher than those experiencing either moderate or low family environment, it can be said that children belonging to *moderate intelligence group* and experiencing Enriched Overall Family Environment are found to exhibit superior School Performance in comparison to children experiencing Moderate Family Environment or Low family environment.

Table 4.26 below shows that the mean school performance scores of enriched family environment group, is 83.00 and that of low family environment group is 65.206, with SDs 12.599 and 10.613 respectively. The obtained 't' value is 5.2094 and this is found to be significant at 0.01 level. Thus it can be inferred that the two groups differ.

Table 4.26
Significance of Difference in Mean School Performance Scores of Elementary School Children Belonging to Low Intellegence at Different Level of *[Overall Family Environment]* (As Perceived by Children)

Groups	*N*	*M*	*S.D*	*t-ratio*	*Level of significance*
Enriched Overall Family Environment	19	83.000	12.599		
Vs				5.2094	0.01
Low Overall Family Environment	34	65.206	14.908		
Enriched Overall Family Environment	19	83.000	12.599		
Vs				2.8451	0.01
Moderate Overall Family Environment	20	70.619	10.613		
Moderate Overall Family Environment	20	70.619	14.908		
Vs				1.4522	NS
Low Overall Family Environment	34	65.206	10.613		

significantly in their school performance. Mean school performance score of enriched family environment is higher than that of low family environment group. The scores indicate that children of low intelligence group experiencing enriched family environment are found to have higher school performance than those experiencing low family environment.

Table 4.26 further shows that mean school performance score of Enriched family environment group is 83.000 and that of moderate family environment group is 70.619, with SDs 12.599 and 14.908 respectively. The obtained 't'value is 2.8451 found to be significant at 0.01 level. It implies that the two groups differ significantly in their school performance. Mean school performance score of enriched family environment is higher than that of moderate family environment group. The scores indicate that children of low intelligence group experiencing enriched family environment are found to have exhibit school performance than those experiencing moderate family environment.

Table 4.26 also reveals that mean school performance score of moderate family environment group is 70.619 and that of low family environment group is 65.200, with SDs 14.908 and 10.613 respectively. The obtained 't' value for these two groups is 1.4522 which is less than the table value, and this is found to be not significant even at .05 level. It means that the two groups do not differ significantly in their school performance.

Since the mean school performance score of children of low group of intelligence experiencing enriched family environment group is higher than that of those experiencing both moderate and low family environment, it can be said that children belonging to *Low Intelligence Group* and experiencing Enriched Overall Family Environment are found to exhibit higher School Performance in comparison to children experiencing Moderate Family Environment and Low family environment.

For a clear comprehension of results comparison for 't'.ratios and mean school performance scores of Tables 4.18, 4.19 and 4.20 are depicted in Table 4.27 and 4.28 respectively.

Tables 4.27 below indicates that significant differences in the mean school performance score of elementary school children at different levels of their family environment are to be seen in the case of *Enriched – Low* and *Enriched – Moderate* family environment groups of children belonging to all the three groups of intelligence i.e. High, *Moderate, and Low intelligence groups,* with respect to *overall family environment* However the same is not found for Moderate – Low family environment group in case of all the three groups of intelligence.

Table 4.27

Comparisons of 't' Ratios, Obtained for School Performance Differential of Elementary School Children Belonging to Similar Intelligence Groups i.e., High; Moderate and Low, at Different Levels of their Family Environment (As Perceived by Children)

Intelligence → *F.E. group ↓*	*High Intelligence*	*Moderate Intelligence*	*Low Intelligence*
Enriched vs Low	3.6839 **	3.7998 **	5.2094 **
Enriched vs Moderate	2.9878 **	3.0659 **	2.8451 **
Moderate vs Low	0.6406	0.5508	1.4522

** Significant at 0.01 level.

Table 4.28

Comparison of Mean School Performance Scores of Elementary School Children Belonging to Similar Intelligence Group i.e. High, Moderate and Low and Experiencing Different Family Environment viz. Enriched, Moderate and Low (As Perceived by Children)

Intelligence → *F.E. group ↓*	*High Intelligence*	*Moderate Intelligence*	*Low Intelligence*
Enriched F.E. group	92.371	89.933	83.000
Moderate F.E. group	79.83	73.813	70.619
Low F.E. group	76.071	70.154	65.209

F.E. - Family Environment.

It can be observed from table 4.28 that mean school performance scores of enriched family environment groups children are higher than that of moderate and low family environment group of children with respect to overall family environment, in case of children belonging to all the three groups of intelligence.

In other words it can be said that children belonging to similar intelligence group, exhibit higher school performance, on experiencing enriched overall family environment than those experiencing moderate and low overall family environment than on experiencing either moderate or low family environment *as perceived by children.*

Therefore Hy 7 of the present study that if a child experiences better family environment (school focussed parent child interaction), *as perceived by children*, then a child will have higher school performance, than a child with *similar intelligence,* experiencing not so good family environment' is retained for *Overall Family Environment,* in case of all the three groups of intelligence i.e. *High; Moderate; and Low intelligence groups* of children, for *Enriched – Low and Enriched – Moderate* family environment groups, but is not retained for Moderate – Low family environment group.

School Performance Differentials in Elementary School Children belonging to Similar Intelligence Group at Different Levels of *Five Dimensions of Family Environment* (as perceived by Children)

School performance differentials in elementary school children belonging to three groups of similar intelligence viz. high, moderate and low intelligence groups, at different level of family environment with respect to five dimensions viz. achievement orientation; cognitive stimulation; recreational orientation; home structure; and language stimulation *as perceived by children* are presented in Tables 4.29- 4.31

Table – 4.29 shows that the mean school performance scores of enriched groups on achievement orientation, cognitive stimulation, recreational orientation, home structure and language stimulation is 88.238, 88.333, 92.258, 88.434 and 92.471 respectively with their SDs 12.415, 13.827, 7.816. 13.17 and 7.232 (Similarly) and that low group on achievement orientation, cognitive stimulation, recreational orientation, home structure and language stimulation is 75.165, 80.125, 77.125, 78.154 and 80.268 respectively with their SDs 16.642, 15.980, 16.848, 13.496 and 16.343. The obtained 't' value between the two groups on achievement orientation, cognitive stimulation, recreational orientation, home structure and language stimulation is 2.5273, 1.7599 3.4081, 2.3768, and 3.0153 respectively and these are found to be significant at 0.01, 0.05, 0.01, 0.05 and 0.01 levels respectively. Thus it can be inferred that the two groups differ significantly in their school performance. Mean school performance score of enriched group on (all the five dimensions) achievement orientation, cognitive stimulation, recreational orientation, home structure and language stimulation is higher than that of their low group. The scores indicate that children of high intelligence group experiencing enriched environment on achievement orientation, cognitive stimulation, recreational orientation, home structure and language stimulation, are found to have higher school performance than those experiencing low environment on the same (dimensions).

Table – 4.29 also shows that the mean school performance scores of enriched groups on achievement orientation, cognitive stimulation, recreational orientation, home structure and language stimulation is 88.238, 88.333, 92.258, 88.434 and 92.471 respectively with their SDs 12.415, 13.827, 7.816, 13.17 and 7.232 (Similarly) and that moderate group on achievement orientation, cognitive stimulation, recreational orientation, home structure and language stimulation is 84.217, 85.444, 82.052, 85.118 and 87.867 respectively with their SDs 14.024, 12.575, 15.422, 15.635 and 10.695. The obtained 't' value between the two groups on achievement orientation, cognitive stimulation, recreational orientation, home structure and language stimulation is 0.9273, 0.7566, 2.7416, 0.7590 and 10.5208 respectively. None of the t. ratios, except for recreational orientation, are found to be significant even at 0.01 level, which is significant at 0.01 level. Thus it can be said that the two groups do not differ significantly in their

Table 4.29

Significance of Difference in Mean School Performance Scores of Elementary School Children Belonging to High Intelligence Group at different Levels of Five Dimensions of Family Environment viz. Achievement Orientation; Cognitive Stimulation; Recreational Orientation; Home Structure; and Language Stimulation ***(As perceived by Children)***

Dimensions of Family Environment	*Family Environment Groups*	*N*	*Mean*	*SD*	*'t' ratios*	*Level of Significance*
Achievement orientation	Enriched	42	88.238	12.415		
	Vs				2.5273	0.01
	Low	12	75.165	16.642		
Cognitive stimulation	Enriched	33	88.333	13.827		
	Vs				1.7599	0.05
	Low	16	80.125	15.980		
Recreational orientation	Enriched	31	92.258	7.816		
	Vs				3.4085	0.01
	Low	16	77.125	16.848		
Home structure	Enriched	37	88.432	13.176		
	Vs				2.3768	0.05
	Low	13	78.154	13.496		
Language stimulation	Enriched	34	92.471	7.232		
	Vs				3.0153	0.01
	Low	18	80.268	16.343		

Contd.

Contd.

Dimensions of Family Environment	*Family Environment Groups*	*N*	*Mean*	*SD*	*'t' ratios*	*Level of Significance*
Achievement orientation	Enriched	42	88.238	12.415	0.9273	NS
	Vs					
	Moderate	13	84.217	14.024		
Cognitive stimulation	Enriched	33	88.333	13.827	0.7566	NS
	Vs					
	Moderate	18	85.444	12.575		
Recreational orientation	Enriched	31	92.258	7.816	2.7416	.01
	Vs					
	Moderate	20	82.050	15.422		
Home structure	Enriched	37	88.432	13.176	0.7590	NS
	Vs					
	Moderate	17	85.118	15.635		
Language stimulation	Enriched	34	92.471	7.232	1.5208	NS
	Vs					
	Moderate	15	87.867	10.695		

Contd.

Contd.

Dimensions of Family Environment	*Family Environment Groups*	*N*	*Mean*	*SD*	*'t' ratios*	*Level of Significance*
Achievement orientation	Moderate	13	84.217	14.024		
	Vs				1.4641	.05
	Low	12	75.165	16.642		
Cognitive stimulation	Moderate	18	85.444	12.575		
	Vs				1.0694	NS
	Low	16	80.125	15.980		
Recreational orientation	Moderate	20	82.050	15.422		
	Vs				0.9047	NS
	Low	16	77.125	16.848		
Home structure	Moderate	17	85.118	15.635		
	Vs				1.3070	NS
	Low	13	78.154	13.496		
Language stimulation	Moderate	15	87.867	10.695		
	Vs				1.6031	NS
	Low	18	80.268	16.343		

school performance except on recreational orientation. Mean school performance score of enriched group on recreational orientation is higher than that of their moderate group. The scores indicate that children of high intelligence group experiencing enriched environment on recreational orientation, are found to have higher school performance than those experiencing moderate environment on the same dimension.

Table – 4.29 further shows that the mean school performance scores of moderate group on achievement orientation, cognitive stimulation, recreational orientation, home structure and language stimulation is 84.217, 85.444, 82.052, 85.118 and 87.867 respectively with their SDs 14.024, 12.575, 15.422, 15.635 and 10.695 and that low group on achievement orientation, cognitive stimulation, recreational orientation, home structure and language stimulation is 75.165, 80.125, 77.125, 78.154 and 80.268 respectively with their SDs 16.642, 15.980, 16.848, 13.496 and 16.343. The obtained 't' value between the two groups on achievement orientation, cognitive stimulation, recreational orientation, home structure and language stimulation is 1.4641, 1.0694, 0.9047, 1.3070 and 1.6031 respectively and the t. ratios obtained for achievement orientation and language stimulation only, are found to be significant at 0.05 and 0.01 level respectively. Thus it can be inferred that the two groups differ significantly in their school performance on achievement orientation and language stimulation. Mean school performance scores of moderate groups on achievement orientation, and language stimulation is higher than that of their low groups. The scores indicate that children of high intelligence group experiencing moderate environment on achievement orientation and language stimulation, are found to exhibit higher school performance than those experiencing low environment on the same dimensions.

Results reveal that the mean school performance score of children of high intelligence group, experiencing enriched family environment is higher than that of those experiencing low family environment on all the five dimensions and also mean school performance score of those experiencing enriched environment on recreational orientation is better than those experiencing moderate family environment on the same. and that of those experiencing moderate family environment on.

Thus it can be said that children of high intelligence group exhibit better school performance on experiencing Enriched Family Environment with respect to all the five dimensions of family environment, i.e., Achievement Orientation, Cognitive Stimulation, Recreational Orientation, Home Structure and Language Stimulation than Low Family Environment with respect to these dimensions.

Results also indicate that children experiencing enriched family environment on recreational orientation exhibit better school performance than those experiencing moderate family environment on the same. However no significant differences are found on all the five dimensions between moderate – low family environment.

Table – 4.30 below shows that the mean school performance scores of enriched groups on achievement orientation, cognitive stimulation, recreational orientation, home structure and language stimulation is 86.368, 85.000, 83.719, 88.000 and 83.316 respectively with their SDs 16.525, 15.969, 16.923, 12.025 and 15.149 (Similarly) and that of low group on achievement orientation, cognitive stimulation, recreational orientation, home structure and language stimulation is 74.500, 72.857, 72.250, 68.215 and73.500 respectively with their SDs 17.483, 17.279, 16.664, 16.738 and 18.184. The obtained 't' values between the two groups on achievement orientation, cognitive stimulation, recreational orientation, home structure and language stimulation is 1.8103, 1.9892, 1.7904, 3.6709 and 1.8351 respectively and these are found to be significant at 0.05, 0.05, 0.05, 0.01and 0.05 levels respectively. Thus it can be inferred that the two groups differ significantly in their school performance. Mean school performance score of enriched group on all the five dimensions viz. achievement orientation, cognitive stimulation, recreational orientation, home structure and language stimulation is higher than that of their low group. The scores indicate that children of moderate intelligence group experiencing enriched environment on achievement orientation, cognitive stimulation, recreational orientation, home structure and language stimulation, are found to exhibit higher school performance than those experiencing low environment on the same dimensions.

Table – 4.30 shows that the mean school performance scores of enriched groups on achievement orientation, cognitive stimulation, recreational orientation, home structure and language stimulation is 86.368, 85.000, 83.719, 88.000 and 83.316 respectively with their SDs 16.525, 15.969, 16.923, 12.025 and 15.149 and that moderate group on achievement orientation, cognitive stimulation, recreational orientation, home structure and language stimulation is 77.917, 75.857, 78.500, 77.071 and 77.800 respectively with their SDs 19.427, 17.594, 17.977, 18.172 and19.477. The obtained 't' value between the two groups on achievement orientation, cognitive stimulation, recreational orientation, home structure and language stimulation is 1.2759, 1.4822, 0.8451, 1.9370 and 0.5882 respectively. None of the t. ratios, except for home structure which is significant at 0.05 level, are found to be significant even at 0.05 level.

Table 4.30

Significance of Difference in Mean School Performance Scores of Elementary School Children Belonging to Moderate Intelligence Group at Different Levels of Five Dimensions of Family Environment viz. Achievement Orientation; Cognitive Stimulation; Recreational Orientation; Home Structure; and Language Stimulation *(As perceived by Children)*

Dimensions of Family Environment	*Family Environment Groups*	*N*	*Mean*	*SD*	*'t' ratios*	*Level of Significance*
Achievement orientation	Enriched	22	86.368	16.525		
	Vs				1.8103	0.05
	Low	10	74.500	17.483		
Cognitive stimulation	Enriched	16	85.000	15.969		
	Vs				1.9892	0.05
	Low	14	72.857	17.279		
Recreational orientation	Enriched	16	83.719	16.923		
	Vs				1.7904	0.05
	Low	12	72.250	16.664		
Home structure	Enriched	16	88.000	12.026		
	Vs				3.6709	0.01
	Low	14	68.214	16.738		

Contd.

Contd.

Dimensions of Family Environment	*Family Environment Groups*	*N*	*Mean*	*SD*	*'t' ratios*	*Level of Significance*
Language stimulation	Enriched	19	83.316	15.149		
	Vs				1.8351	0.05
	Low	20	73.500	18.184		
Achievement orientation	Enriched	22	86.368	16.525		
	Vs				1.2759	NS
	Moderate	12	77.917	19.427		
Cognitive stimulation	Enriched	16	85.000	75.857		
	Vs				1.4822	NS
	Moderate	14	15.969	17.594		
Recreational orientation	Enriched	16	83.719	16.923		
	Vs				0.8451	NS
	Moderate	16	78.500	17.977		
Home structure	Enriched	16	88.000	12.026		
	Vs				1.9133	0.05
	Moderate	14	77.071	18.172		

Contd.

Contd.

Dimensions of Family Environment	*Family Environment Groups*	*N*	*Mean*	*SD*	*'t' ratios*	*Level of Significance*
Language stimulation	Enriched	19	83.316	15.149		
	Vs				0.5882	NS
	Moderate	5	77.800	19.477		
Achievement orientation	Moderate	12	77.917	74.500	0.4339	NS
	Vs					
	Low	10	19.427	17.483		
Cognitive stimulation	Moderate	14	75.857	17.594		
	Vs				0.4552	NS
	Low	14	72.857	17.279		
Recreational orientation	Moderate	16	78.500	72.250		
	Vs				0.9489	NS
	Low	12	17.997	16.664		
Home structure	Moderate	14	77.071	68.214		
	Vs				1.3414	NS
	Low	14	18.172	16.738		
Language stimulation	Moderate	5	77.800	19.477		
	Vs				0.4473	NS
	Low	20	73.500	18.184		

Thus it can be said that the two groups do not differ significantly in their school performance except on home structure. Mean school performance score of enriched group on home structure is higher than that of their moderate group. The scores indicate that children of moderate intelligence group experiencing enriched environment on home structure are found to exhibit higher school performance than those experiencing moderate family environment on the same.

Table – 4.30 further shows that the mean school performance scores of moderate group on achievement orientation, cognitive stimulation, recreational orientation, home structure and language stimulation is is 77.917, 75.857, 78.500, 77.071 and 77.800 respectively with their SDs 19.427, 17.594, 17.977, 18.172 and 19.477 and that of low group on achievement orientation, cognitive stimulation, recreational orientation, home structure and language stimulation is 74.500, 72.857, 72.250, 68.215 and 73.500 respectively with their SDs 17.483, 17.279, 16.664, 16.738 and 18.184.The obtained 't' value between the two groups on achievement orientation, cognitive stimulation, recreational orientation, home structure and language stimulation is 0.4339, 0.4552, 0.9482, 1.3414 and 0.4473 respectively and these are found to be not significant even at 0.05 level. Thus it can be inferred that the two groups do not differ significantly in their school performance on any of the dimensions.

Scores reveal that the mean school performance score of children of *moderate intelligence group*, experiencing enriched family environment is higher than that of those experiencing low family environment on all the five dimensions and also mean school performance score of those experiencing enriched environment on home structure is higher than those experiencing moderate family environment on the same.

Thus it can be said that children belonging to moderate intelligence group exhibit better school performance on experiencing enriched family environment with respect to all the five dimensions of family environment i.e. achievement orientation, cognitive stimulation, recreational orientation, home structure and language stimulation than low family environment with respect to these dimensions as perceived by *Children.*

Results also indicate that children experiencing enriched family environment on home structure exhibit better school performance than those experiencing moderate family environment on the same.

However no significant differences are found on all the five dimensions between moderate – low family environment.

Table – 4.31 shows that in case of children belonging to low intelligence group the mean school performance scores of enriched groups

Table 4.31

Significance of Difference in Mean School Performance Scores of Elementary School Children Belonging to Low Intelligence Group at Different Levels of Five Dimensions of Family Environment viz. Achievement Orientation; Cognitive Stimulation; Recreational Orientation; Home Structure; and Language Stimulation

(As perceived by Children)

Dimensions of Family Environment	*Family Environment Groups*	*N*	*Mean*	*SD*	*'t' ratios*	*Level of Significance*
Achievement orientation	Enriched	27	79.593	14.124		
	Vs				4.1948	0.01
	Low	30	64.864	12.168		
Cognitive stimulation	Enriched	19	80.316	13.635		
	Vs				3.7219	0.01
	Low	30	66.500	10.948		
Recreational orientation	Enriched	23	80.000	13.831		
	Vs				3.9160	0.01
	Low	26	65.654	11.519		
Home structure	Enriched	24	80.417	13.886		
	Vs				4.0397	0.01
	Low	31	66.323	11.326		

Contd.

Contd.

Dimensions of Family Environment	*Family Environment Groups*	*N*	*Mean*	*SD*	*'t' ratios*	*Level of Significance*
Language stimulation	Enriched	26	83.077	12.517		
	Vs				6.1600	0.01
	Low	37	64.636	10.407		
Achievement orientation	Enriched	27	79.593	14.124		
	Vs				2.5385	0.01
	Moderate	17	69.529	11.897		
Cognitive stimulation	Enriched	19	80.316	13.635		
	Vs				2.2890	0.05
	Moderate	25	70.240	15.485		
Recreational orientation	Enriched	23	80.000	13.831		
	Vs				2.6927	0.01
	Moderate	25	69.200	13.937		
Home structure	Enriched	24	80.417	13.886		
	Vs				2.8932	0.01
	Moderate	19	67.947	14.151		

Contd.

Contd.

Dimensions of Family Environment	*Family Environment Groups*	*N*	*Mean*	*SD*	*'t' ratios*	*Level of Significance*
Language stimulation	Enriched	26	83.077	12.517		
	Vs				3.9839	0.01
	Moderate	11	65.027	12.629		
Achievement orientation	Moderate	17	69.529	11.897		
	Vs				1.2804	NS
	Low	30	64.867	12.168		
Cognitive stimulation	Moderate	25	70.240	15.485		
	Vs				1.0147	NS
	Low	30	66.500	10.948		
Recreational orientation	Moderate	25	69.200	13.937		
	Vs				0.9884	NS
	Low	26	65.654	11.519		

Contd.

Contd.

Dimensions of Family Environment	*Family Environment Groups*	*N*	*Mean*	*SD*	*'t' ratios*	*Level of Significance*
Home structure	Moderate	19	67.947	14.151		
	Vs				0.4241	NS
	Low	31	66.323	11.326		
Language stimulation	Moderate	11	65.029	12.629		
	Vs				0.0936	NS
	Low	37	64.636	10.407		

on achievement orientation, cognitive stimulation, recreational orientation, home structure and language stimulation is 79.593, 80.316, 80.000, 80.417 and 83.077 respectively with their SDs 14.124, 13.635, 13.831, 13.886 and 12.517 respectively and that low group on achievement orientation, cognitive stimulation, recreational orientation, home structure and language stimulation is 64.867, 66.500, 65.654, 66.323 and 65.027 respectively with their SDs 12.168, 10.948, 11.519, 11.326 and 10.407 respectively. The obtained 't' values between the two groups on achievement orientation, cognitive stimulation, recreational orientation, home structure and language stimulation are 4.1948, 3.7219, 3.9160, 4.0397 and 6.0323 respectively and all these are found to be significant at 0.01 level. Thus it can be inferred that the two groups differ significantly in their school performance. Mean school performance scores of enriched groups on all the five dimensions is higher than that of their low group. The scores indicate that children of low intelligence group experiencing enriched environment on achievement orientation, cognitive stimulation, recreational orientation, home structure and language stimulation, are found to have higher school performance than those belonging to Low groups of the same dimensions.

Table – 4.31 also shows that for low intelligence group of children the mean school performance scores of enriched groups on achievement orientation, cognitive stimulation, recreational orientation, home structure and language stimulation is 79.593, 80.316, 80.000, 80.417 and 83.077 respectively with their SDs 14.124, 13.635, 13.831, 13.886 and 12.517 and that of moderate group on achievement orientation, cognitive stimulation, recreational orientation, home structure and language stimulation is 69.529, 70.240, 69.200, 67.947 and 64.636 respectively with their SDs 11.897, 13.635, 13.831, 14.151 and 12.629. The obtained 't' value between the two groups on achievement orientation, cognitive stimulation, recreational orientation, home structure and language stimulation is 2.5385, 2.2890, 2.6927, 2.8932 and 4.1702 respectively and all these values are found to be significant at 0.01, 0.05, 0.01, 0.01 and 0.01 levels respectively. Thus it can be said that the two groups differ significantly in their school performance on all the five dimensions of family environment. Mean school performance score of enriched group on achievement orientation, cognitive stimulation, recreational orientation, home structure and language stimulation is higher than that of their moderate group. The scores indicate that children belonging to Enriched groups of all the five dimensions are found to have higher school performance than those belonging to Moderate groups of the same (dimension).

Table–4.31 further shows that the mean school performance scores of moderate group on achievement orientation, cognitive stimulation, recreational orientation, home structure and language stimulation is 69.529, 70.240, 69.200, 67.947 and 64.636 respectively with their SDs 11.897, 13.635, 13.831, 14.151 and12.629. and that low group on achievement orientation, cognitive stimulation, recreational orientation, home structure and language stimulation is 64.867, 66.500, 65.654, 66.323 and 65.027 respectively with their SDs 12.168, 10.948, 11.519, 11.326 and 10.407 respectively. The obtained 't' value between the two groups on achievement orientation, cognitive stimulation, recreational orientation, home structure and language stimulation is 1.2804, 1.0147, 0.9884, 0.4241 and 0.0936 respectively and none of the t. values are found to be significant even at 0.05 level. Thus it can be inferred that the two groups do not differ significantly in their school performance on all the five dimensions of family environment.

Results reveal that the mean school performance score of children of high intelligence group, experiencing enriched family environment is higher than that of those experiencing both moderate and low family environment on all the five dimensions.

Thus it can be said that children belonging to low intelligence group exhibit higher school performance on experiencing Enriched family environment with respect to all the five dimensions of family environment i.e. achievement orientation, cognitive stimulation, recreational orientation, home structure and language stimulation than those experiencing both Moderate and Low family environment with respect to these five dimensions. However no significant differences are found on any of the five dimensions between moderate – low family environment.

For a clear comprehension of results comparison for 't'.ratios and mean school performance scores of Tables nos. 4.29,4.30 and 4.31 are depicted in Table no. 4.32 and 4.33 respectively.

Tables 4.32 below indicates that significant differences in the mean school performance score of elementary school children at different levels of their family environment are to be seen in the case of *Enriched – Low* family environment groups of children belonging to al the three groups of intelligence i.e. *High, Moderate, and Low intelligence groups*, with respect to all the five dimensions viz. Achievement orientation, Cognitive stimulation, Recreational orientation, Home structure and Language stimulation. However the same is not found for Moderate – Low family environment group in case of all the three groups of intelligence.

Table 4.32

Comparisons of 't' Ratios Obtained for School Performance Differentials of Elementary School Children Belonging to Similar Intelligence Group viz. High, Moderate and Low, at Different Levels of Family Environment i.e., Enriched, Moderate and Low with Respect to all the Five Dimension of Family Environment. (As Perceived by Children)

Intelligence group → *Dimensions of F.E.*	*Levels of F.E.*	*High Intelligence*	*Moderate Intelligence*	*Low Intelligence*
AO	En vs Lo	2.5273 **	1.8103 *	4.1948 **
	En vs Mo	0.9273	1.2759	2.5385 **
	Mo vs Lo	1.4641	0.4339	1.2804
CS	En vs Lo	1.7599 *	1.9892 *	3.7219 **
	En vs Mo	0.7566	1.4822	2.2890 **
	Mo vs Lo	1.0694	0.4552	1.0147
RO	En vs Lo	3.4085 **	1.7904 *	3.9160 **
	En vs Mo	2.7416**	0.8451	2.6927 **
	Mo vs Lo	0.9047	0.9489	0.9884
HS	En vs Lo	2.3768 *	3.6709 **	4.4340 **
	En vs Mo	0.7590	1.9370 *	2.6358**
	Mo vs Lo	1.3020	1.3414	0.4241
LS	En vs Lo	3.0153 **	1.8351 *	6.1600 **
	En vs Mo	1.5208	0.5882	3.9839 **
	Mo vs Lo	1.6031	0.4473	0.0936

** Significant at .01 level; * Significant at 0.05 level

AO = Achievement Orientation; CS = Cognitive Stimulation
RO = Recreated Orientation; HS = Home Structure
LS = Language Stimulation; F.E- Family Environment
En – Enriched; Mo – Moderate; Lo – Low.

Table 4.33

Comparison of Mean School Performance Scores of Elementary School Children Belonging to Similar Intelligence Group viz. High, Moderate and Low, and Experiencing Different Family Environment i.e., Enriched, Moderate and Low with Respect to Five Dimension of Family Environment (As Perceived by Children)

Intelligence group → *Dimensions of F.E.*	*Levels of F.E.*	*High Intelligence*	*Moderate Intelligence*	*Low Intelligence*
AO	Enriched	88.238	86.368	79.593
	Moderate	84.217	77.917	69.529
	Low	75.165	74.500	64.867
CS	Enriched	88.333	85.000	80.316
	Moderate	85.444	75.857	70.240
	Low	80.125	72.857	66.500
RO	Enriched	92.258	83.719	80.000
	Moderate	82.050	78.500	69.200
	Low	77.125	72.250	65.657
HS	Enriched	88.434	88.000	80.417
	Moderate	85.118	77.071	67.947
	Low	78.154	68.214	66.323
LS	Enriched	92.471	83.316	83.077
	Moderate	87.867	77.800	65.027
	Low	80.268	73.500	64.636

F.E. = Family Environment; AO = Achievement Orientation
CS = Cognitive Stimulation; RO = Recreated Orientation
HS = Home Structure; LS = Language Stimulation

It can be observed from table 4.33 that mean school performance scores of similar intelligence group of children, experiencing enriched family environment on all the five dimensions viz achievement orientation, cognitive stimulation, recreational orientation, home structure and language stimulation are higher than that of those experiencing low family environment on these dimensions. It is also observed that mean school performance scores of children experiencing enriched family environment is higher than that of those experiencing moderate family environment on recreational orientation in case of high intelligence group of children; on home structure in case of moderate intelligence group of children and on all the five dimensions in case of low intelligence group of children.

In other words it can be said that children belonging to similar intelligence group, exhibit higher school performance, on experiencing *Enriched family environment* on *all the five dimensions* of family environment than those experiencing *Low Family Environment* on the same. Also children experiencing *Enriched Family Environment* are found to exhibit higher school performance than those experiencing Moderate Family Environment on *recreational orientation* in case of children of *high intelligence group*; on *home structure* incase of children of *moderate intelligence* group and on *all the five dimensions* in case of children of *low intelligence group.*

Therefore Hy 7 of the present study that 'if a child experiences better family environment (school focussed parent child interaction), *as perceived by children*, then a child will have higher school performance, than a child with *similar intelligence,* experiencing not so good family environment' is retained at :-

Enriched – Low level for children of all the three groups of intelligence i.e. *High, Moderate; and Low intelligence* on all the five dimensions viz *achievement orientation, cognitive stimulation, recreational orientation, home structure and language stimulation.*

Enriched - Moderate level for children of *high intelligence* on *recreational orientation*; for children of *moderate intelligence* on *home structure*; and for children of *low intelligence* on *all the five dimensions*

School Performance Differentials in Elementary School Children belonging to Similar Intelligence Group at Different Levels of *Overall Family Environment* (as perceived by Parents).

School performance differentials in elementary school children belonging to three groups of similar intelligence viz. high; middle and low intelligence group, at different levels of Overall Family environment as perceived by children are presented in Tables 4.34-4.36.

Table 4.34 below shows that the mean school performance score of enriched overall family environment group, is 90.667 and that of low family environment group is 78.733, with SDs 9.526 and 15.872 respectively. The obtained 't' value is 2.6580 and this is found to be significant at 0.01 level. Thus it can be inferred that the two groups differ significantly in their school performance. The mean school performance score of enriched overall family environment group of children belonging to high intelligence group is higher than that of low overall family environment group. The scores indicate that children belonging to Enriched overall family environment (high intelligence group) are found to have higher school performance than those belonging to Low overall family environment group.

Table 4.34 further shows that mean school performance score of enriched overall family environment group is 90.667 and that of moderate overall family environment group is 85.273, with SDs 9.526 and 15.838 respectively. The obtained 't' value is 1.4039, and this is found to be not significant even at .05. It implies that the two groups do not differ significantly in their school performance.

Table 4.34

Significance of Difference in Mean School Performance Scores of Elementary School Children Belonging to High Intelligence Group at Different Levels of *Overall Family Environment* (As Perceived by Parents)

Groups	*N*	*M*	*S.D*	*t-ratio*	*Level of significance*
Enriched Overall Family Environment	27	90.667	9.526		
Vs				2.6580	0.01
Low Overall Family Environment	15	78.733	15.872		
Enriched Overall Family Environment	27	90.667	9.526		
Vs				1.4039	NS
Moderate Overall Family Environment	22	85.273	15.838		
Moderate Overall Family Environment	22	85.273	15.838		
Vs				1.2315	NS
Low Overall Family Environment	15	78.733	15.872		

Table 4.34 indicates that mean school performance score of moderate overall family environment group is 85.273 and that of low overall family environment group is 78.733, with SDs 15.838 and 15.872 respectively. The obtained 't' value for these two groups is 1.2315, which is less than the table value and this is found to be not significant even at .05. It means that the two groups do not differ significantly in their school performance.

Since the mean school performance score of children belonging to enriched family environment group is higher than that of both moderate and low family environment group of children having similar intelligence, it can be said that children belonging to *high intelligence group* and experiencing Enriched Overall Family Environment are found to exhibit higher School Performance in comparison to children experiencing Moderate and Low Overall Family Environment having similar intelligence.

Table 4.35

Significance of Difference in Mean School Performance Scores of Elementary School Children with Similar Intelligence Moderate Intelligence at Different Levels of *Overall Family Environment* (As Perceived by Parents)

Groups	*N*	*M*	*S.D*	*t-ratio*	*Level of significance*
Enriched Overall Family Environment	17	85.267	12.318		
Vs				3.5393	0.01
Low Overall Family Environment	12	69.825	11.016		
Enriched Overall Family Environment	17	85.267	12.318		
Vs				1.6300	NS
Moderate Overall Family Environment	23	77.391	18.211		
Moderate Overall Family Environment	23	77.391	18.211		
Vs				1.5276	NS
Low Overall Family Environment	12	69.825	11.016		

Table 4.35 shows that the mean school performance score of enriched overall family environment group, is 85.267 and that of low family

environment group is 69.825, with SDs 12.318 and 11.016 respectively. The obtained 't' value is 3.5393 and this is found to be significant at 0.01. Thus it can be inferred that the two groups differ significantly in their school performance. The mean school performance score of enriched overall family environment group of children belonging to moderate intelligence group is higher than that of low overall family environment group. The scores indicate that children belonging to Enriched overall family environment (moderate intelligence group) are found to have higher school performance than those belonging to Low overall family environment group.

Table 4.35 further shows that mean school performance score of enriched overall family environment group is 85.267 and that of moderate overall family environment group is 77.391, with SDs 12.318 and 18.211 respectively. The obtained 't'value is 1.6300, which is less than table value and this is found to be not significant even at 0.05. It implies that the two groups do not differ significantly in their school performance.

Table 4.35 that mean school performance score of moderate overall family environment group is 77.391 and that of low overall family environment group is 69.825, with SDs 18.211 and 11.016 respectively. The obtained 't' value for these two groups is 1.5276, and this is found to be not significant even at 0.05 level. It means that the two groups do not differ significantly in their school performance.

Since the mean school performance scores of children of moderate intelligence group experiencing enriched overall family environment is higher than that of those experiencing low overall family environment, it can be said that children belonging to *moderate intelligence group* and experiencing Enriched Overall Family Environment are found to exhibit higher School Performance in comparison to children experiencing Low Overall Family Environment.

Table 4.36 below shows that in case of children belonging to low intelligence group, the mean school performance score of enriched overall family environment group, is 84.294 and that of low family environment group is 60.261, with SDs 9.476 and 9.988 respectively. The obtained 't' value is 7.4798 and this is found to be significant at 0.01. Thus it can be inferred that the two groups differ significantly in their school performance. The mean school performance score of enriched overall family environment group of children (low intelligence group) is higher than that of low overall family environment group. The scores indicate that children belonging to Enriched overall family environment (low intelligence group) are found to have higher school performance than those belonging to Low overall family environment group.

Table 4.36 further shows that mean school performance score of enriched overall family environment group is 84.294 and that of moderate overall family environment group is 74.048, with SDs 9.476 and 11.328

Table 4.36

Significance of Difference in Mean School Performance Scores of Elementary School Children with Similar Intelligence Low Intelligence at Different Level of *Overall Family Environment* (As Perceived by Parents)

Groups	*N*	*M*	*S.D*	*t-ratio*	*Level of significance*
Enriched Overall Family Environment	15	84.294	9.476		
Vs				7.4798	0.01
Low Overall Family Environment	23	60.261	9.988		
Enriched Overall Family Environment	15	84.294	9.476		
Vs				2.9459	0.01
Moderate Overall Family Environment	21	74.048	11.328		
Moderate Overall Family Environment	21	74.048	11.328		
Vs				4.2652	0.01
Low Overall Family Environment	23	60.261	9.988		

respectively. The obtained 't' value is 2.9459, and this is found to be significant at 0.01. It implies that the two groups differ significantly in their school performance. Mean school performance score of enriched overall family environment is higher than that of moderate overall family environment group. The scores indicate that children coming from Enriched overall family environment (low intelligence group) are found to have higher school performance than those belonging to Moderate family environment group.

Table 4.36 indicates that mean school performance score of moderate overall family environment group is 74.048 and that of low overall family environment group is 60.261, with SDs 11.328 and 9.988 respectively. The obtained 't' value for these two groups is 4.2652, this is found to be significant at 0.01. It means that the two groups differ significantly in their school performance. The mean school performance score of enriched overall family environment group of children (low intelligence group) is higher than that of low overall family environment group. The scores indicate that children belonging to Enriched overall family environment (low intelligence group) are found to have higher school performance than those belonging to Low overall family environment group.

Since the mean school performance score of children experiencing enriched family environment group is higher than that of both moderate and low family environment group of children having similar intelligence, it can be said that children belonging to *low intelligence group* and experiencing Enriched Overall Family Environment are found to have superior School Performance in comparison to children experiencing either Moderate Family Environment or Low family environment. In addition to this it can also be said that children experiencing Moderate Overall Family Environment are found to have superior School Performance in comparison to children experiencing Low Overall Family Environment.

For a clear comprehension of results comparisons for 't' ratios and mean school performance of table no. 4.34, 4.35 and 4.36 are presented in tables 4.37 and 4.38.

Table 4.37 below indicates that significant differences in the mean school performance score of elementary school children at different levels of their family environment (as perceived by *Parents*) are to be seen in the case of *Enriched – Low* family environment groups of children belonging to al the three groups of intelligence i.e. *High, Moderate, and Low intelligence groups,* with respect to overall family environment. Such differences are also found between *Enriched – Moderate and Moderate – Low* family environment group in case of low intelligence group of children However the same is not found for Moderate – Low family environment group in case of all the three groups of intelligence.

It can be observed from table 4.38 that mean school performance scores enriched family environment group of children are higher than that of low family environment group of children of all the three groups of intelligence. It is also observed that in case of children of low intelligence group mean school performance of children experiencing enriched family environment is higher than that of those experiencing moderate family environ and children experiencing moderate family environment exhibit high mean school performance score than those experiencing low family environment with respect to overall family environment as perceived by parent.

Table 4.37

Comparisons of 't' Ratio, Obtained for School Performance Differentials of Elementary School Children Belonging to Similar Intelligence Groups i.e., High; Moderate and Low Intelligence, at Different Level of Family Environment, with Respect to Overall Family Environment (As Perceived by Parents)

Intelligence → *F.E. group ↓*	*High Intelligence*	*Moderate Intelligence*	*Low Intelligence*
Enriched vs Low	4.490 **	3.5393 **	7.4798 **
Enriched vs Moderate	1.4039	1.6300	2.9459 **
Moderate vs Low	1.2315	1.5276	4.2652 **

** Significant at .01 level.

Table 4.38

Comparison of Mean School Performance Scores of Elementary School Children Belonging to Similar Intelligence Group i.e., High, Moderate and Low and Experiencing Different Family Environment viz. Enriched, Moderate and Low. (As Perceived by Parents)

Intelligence → *F.E. group ↓*	*High Intelligence*	*Moderate Intelligence*	*Low Intelligence*
Enriched Family Environment group	90.667	85.267	84.294
Moderate F.E. group	85.273	77.391	74.048
Low F.E. group	78.733	69.825	60.261

In other words it can be said that children belonging to similar intelligence group, exhibit higher school performance, on experiencing Enriched family environment those experiencing Low Family Environment with respect to overall family environment. Whereas in case of children of low intelligence group it can be said that children experiencing enriched family environment are found to exhibit high school performance than those experiencing moderate family environment and also children experiencing moderate family environment exhibit higher school performance than those experiencing low family environment, with respect to overall family environment as perceived by parents

Therefore Hy 8 of the present study that ' if a child experiences better family environment (school focussed parent child interaction), *as perceived by Parents*, then a child will have higher school performance than a child with *similar intelligence,* experiencing not so good family environment' is retained with respect to *overall family environment* at :-

Enriched – Low level for children of all the three groups of intelligence i.e. *High, Moderate; and Low intelligence groups.*

Enriched - Moderate level and *Moderate – low* level for children of *low intelligence group.*

School Performance Differentials in Elementary School Children belonging to Similar Intelligence Group at Different Levels of *Five Dimensions of Family Environment* as Perceived by Parents

School performance differentials in elementary school children belonging to three groups of similar intelligence viz. high, moderate and low intelligence groups, at different level of family environment with respect to five dimensions viz. achievement orientation; cognitive stimulation; recreational orientation; home structure; and language stimulation *as perceived by parents* are presented in table 4.39 - 4.41

Table – 4.39 ahead shows that the mean school performance scores of enriched groups on achievement orientation, cognitive stimulation, recreational orientation, home structure and language stimulation are 91.059, 90.621, 88.969, 87.952 and 96.524 respectively with their SDs 8.585, 9.568, 12.353, 14.209 and 15.290 (Similarly) and that low group on achievement orientation, cognitive stimulation, recreational orientation, home structure and language stimulation is 78.882, 79.368, 79.750, 78.083 and 78.452 respectively with their SDs 18.717, 17.592, 16.318, 14.665 and 13.501. The obtained 't' value between the two groups on achievement orientation, cognitive stimulation, recreational orientation, home structure and language stimulation is 2.2567, 2.5517, 2.1679, 2.0700 and 1.8953 respectively and all these values, except for recreational orientation which is significant at 0.01 level, are found to be significant at 0.05 level. Thus it can be inferred that the two groups differ significantly in their school performance. Mean school performance score of enriched group on achievement orientation, cognitive stimulation, recreational orientation, home structure and language stimulation is higher than that of their low group. The scores indicate that children of high intelligence experiencing enriched environment on achievement orientation, cognitive stimulation, recreational orientation, home structure and language stimulation, are found to exhibit higher school performance than those experiencing low environment on the same dimensions.

Table 4.39

Significance of Difference in Mean School Performance Scores of Elementary School Children Belonging to High Intelligence Group at Different Levels of Five Dimensions of Family Environment viz. Achievement Orientation; Cognitive Stimulation; Recreational Orientation; Home Structure; and Language Stimulation (As Perceived by Parents)

Dimensions of Family Environment	*Family Enviro-nment Groups*	*N*	*Mean*	*SD*	*'t' ratios*	*Level of Significance*
Achievement	Enriched	34	91.059	8.585		
orientation	Vs				2.2567	0.05
	Low	13	78.882	18.717		
Cognitive	Enriched	29	90.621	9.568		
stimulation	Vs				2.5517	0.01
	Low	19	79.368	17.592		
Recreational	Enriched	32	88.969	79.368		
orientation	Vs				2.1679	0.05
	Low	20	12.353	16.318		
Home	Enriched	42	87.952	14.209		
structure	Vs				2.0700	0.05
	Low	12	78.083	14.665		
Language	Enriched	21	86.524	15.290		
stimulation	Vs				1.8953	0.05
	Low	26	78.452	13.501		
Achievement	Enriched	34	91.059	8.585		

Contd

Contd.

Dimensions of Family Environment	*Family Enviro-nment Groups*	*N*	*Mean*	*SD*	*'t' ratios*	*Level of Significance*
orientation	Vs				2.3283	0.05
	Moderate	17	82.154	14.554		
Cognitive	Enriched	29	90.621	9.568		
stimulation	Vs				1.2870	NS
	Moderate	16	85.563	14.022		
Recreational	Enriched	32	88.969	12.353		
orientation	Vs				0.0930	NS
	Moderate	12	88.583	12.203		
Home	Enriched	42	87.952	14.209		
structure	Vs				0.1360	NS
	Moderate	10	87.400	10.707		
Language	Enriched	21	86.524	15.290		
stimulation	Vs				0.5402	NS
	Moderate	17	83.941	13.501		
Achievement	Moderate	17	82.154	14.554		
orientation	Vs				0.5213	NS
	Low	13	78.882	18.717		
Cognitive	Moderate	16	85.563	14.022		
stimulation	Vs				1.1587	NS
	Low	19	79.368	17.592		
Recreational	Moderate	12	88.583	12.203		
orientation	Vs				1.7416	.05
	Low	20	79.750	16.318		
Home	Moderate	10	87.400	10.707		
structure	Vs				1.7186	NS
	Low	12	78.083	14.665		
Language	Moderate	17	83.941	14.119		
stimulation	Vs				0.6978	NS
	Low	26	78.452	13.501		

Table – 4.39 also shows that the mean school performance scores of enriched groups on achievement orientation, cognitive stimulation, recreational orientation, home structure and language stimulation is 91.059, 90.621, 88.969, 87.952 and 96.524 respectively with their SDs 8.585, 9.568, 12.353, 14.209 and 15.290 (Similarly) and that moderate group on achievement orientation, cognitive stimulation, recreational orientation, home structure and language stimulation 82.154, 85.623, 88.583, 87.400 and 83.941 with their SDs 14.554, 14.022, 12.203, 10.707 and 14.119.The obtained 't' value between the two groups on achievement orientation, cognitive stimulation, recreational orientation, home structure and language stimulation is 2.3283, 1.2870, .0930, 0.1360 and 0.5402 respectively. The 't'. value for achievement orientation is found to be significant at 0.05 level and all other four dimensions are not found to be significant even at 0.05 level. Thus it can be said that the two groups do not differ significantly in their school performance except on achievement orientation. Mean school performance score of enriched group on achievement orientation is higher than that of their moderate group. The scores indicate that children of high intelligence experiencing enriched environment on achievement orientation are found to have higher school performance than those belonging to moderate group of the same dimension.

Table –4.39 further shows that the mean school performance scores of moderate group on achievement orientation, cognitive stimulation, recreational orientation, home structure and language stimulation is 82.154. 85.623, 88.583, 87.400 and 83.941 with their SDs 14.544, 14.022, 12.203, 10.707 and 14.119. Similarly and that low group on achievement orientation, cognitive stimulation, recreational orientation, home structure and language stimulation is 82.154, 79.368, 79.750, 78.083 and 86.962 respectively with their SDs 14.154, 17.592, 16.318, 14.665 and 13.501. The obtained 't' value between the two groups on achievement orientation, cognitive stimulation, recreational orientation, home structure and language stimulation is 0.5385, 1.!587, 1.7416, 1.7186 and 0.6978 respectively and the t. ratio obtained for only recreational orientation is found to be significant at 0.05 level. Thus it can be inferred that the two groups differ significantly in their school performance on recreational orientation. Mean school performance scores of moderate groups on recreational orientation, is higher than that of their low groups. The scores indicate that children of high intelligence experiencing moderate environment on recreational orientation are found to have higher school performance than those experiencing low environment on the same dimension.

Results reveal that the mean school performance score of children of high intelligence group, experiencing enriched family environment is higher than that of those experiencing low family environment on all the five dimensions. Mean school performance score of those experiencing enriched environment on recreational orientation is higher than those experiencing moderate family environment on the same and also those experiencing moderate environment have higher mean school performance score than those experiencing low family environment on recreational orientation and home structure.

Thus results indicate that children belonging to high intelligence group exhibit better school performance on experiencing enriched family environment with respect to all the five dimensions of family environment i.e. achievement orientation, cognitive stimulation, recreational orientation, home structure and language stimulation than low family environment with respect to these dimensions.

Results also indicate that children experiencing enriched family environment on recreational orientation exhibit better school performance than those experiencing moderate family environment on the same.

Further results also indicate that in case of recreational orientation and home structure, children experiencing moderate family environment exhibit better school performance than those experiencing low family environment.

Table 4.40

Significance of Difference in Mean School Performance Scores of Elementary School Children Belonging to Moderate Intelligence Group at Different Levels of Five Dimensions of Family Environment viz. Achievement Orientation; Cognitive Stimulation; Recreational Orientation; Home Structure; and Language Stimulation (As Perceived by Parents)

Dimensions Of Family Environment	*Family Environment Groups*	*N*	*Mean*	*SD*	*'t' ratios*	*Level of Significance*
Achievement orientation	Enriched	25	83.840	14.775		
	Vs				6.6126	0.01
	Low	10	60.300	6.278		
Cognitive stimulation	Enriched	24	82.542	14.720		
	Vs				4.5763	0.01
	Low	14	63.268	11.022		
Recreational orientation	Enriched	19	81.684	13.298		
	Vs				2.4922	0.01
	Low	13	68.077	16.932		
Home structure	Enriched	27	82.667	14.689		
	Vs				2.9732	0.01
	Low	13	66.750	16.391		

(contd.)

Contd.

Dimensions Of Family Environment	*Family Environment Groups*	*N*	*Mean*	*SD*	*'t' ratios*	*Level of Significance*
Language stimulation	Enriched	22	85.455	12.220		
	Vs				4.5097	0.01
	Low	17	65.882	14.311		
Achievement orientation	Enriched	25	83.840	14.775		
	Vs				1.8649	0.05
	Moderate	17	74.176	17.551		
Cognitive stimulation	Enriched	24	82.542	14.720		
	Vs				0.7666	NS
	Moderate	14	78.071	18.699		
Recreational orientation	Enriched	19	81.684	13.298		
	Vs				1.0879	NS
	Moderate	20	76.150	18.205		
Home structure	Enriched	27	82.667	14.689		
	Vs				2.0399	0.05
	Moderate	12	71.308	16.619		
Language stimulation	Enriched	22	85.455	12.220		
	Vs				1.9886	0.05
	Moderate	13	73.846	18.835		
Achievement orientation	Moderate	17	74.176	17.551		
	Vs				2.9544	0.05
	Low	10	60.300	6.278		
Cognitive stimulation	Moderate	14	78.071	18.699		
	Vs				2.5488	0.01
	Low	14	63.286	11.022		
Recreational orientation	Moderate	20	76.150	18.205		
	Vs				1.2990	NS
	Low	13	68.077	16.932		
Home structure	Moderate	12	71.308	16.619		
	Vs				0.6896	NS
	Low	13	66.750	16.391		
Language stimulation	Moderate	13	73.846	18.835		
	Vs				1.2698	NS
	Low	17	65.882	14.311		

Table – 4.40 shows that the mean school performance scores of enriched groups on achievement orientation, cognitive stimulation, recreational orientation, home structure and language stimulation is 83.840, 82.542, 81.684, 82.667 and 85.455 respectively with their SDs 14.775, 14.720,

13.928, 14.689 and 12.220 respectively. (Similarly) and that low group on achievement orientation, cognitive stimulation, recreational orientation, home structure and language stimulation is 60.300, 63.268, 68.077, 66.750 and 65.882 respectively with their SDs 6.278, 11.022, 16.932, 16.391 and14.311. The obtained 't' value between the two groups on achievement orientation, cognitive stimulation, recreational orientation, home structure and language stimulation is 6.6126, 4.5763, 2.4299, 2.9732 and 4.5097 respectively and these are found to be significant at 0.01, 0.01, 0.05, 0.01 and 0.01 levels respectively. Thus it can be inferred that the two groups differ significantly in their school performance. Mean school performance score of enriched group on all the five dimensions viz. achievement orientation, cognitive stimulation, recreational orientation, home structure and language stimulation is higher than that of their low group. The scores indicate that children moderate intelligence group experiencing enriched environment on achievement orientation, cognitive stimulation, recreational orientation, home structure and language stimulation, are found to exhibit higher school performance than those experiencing low environment on the same dimensions.

Table – 4.40 also shows that the mean school performance scores of enriched groups on achievement orientation, cognitive stimulation, recreational orientation, home structure and language stimulation is 83.840, 82.542, 81.684, 82.667 and 85.455 respectively with their SDs 14.775, 14.720, 13.928, 14.689 and 12.220 and that moderate group on achievement orientation, cognitive stimulation, recreational orientation, home structure and language stimulation is 74.176, 78.071, 76.150, 71.308 and 73.846 respectively with their SDs 17.551, 18.699, 18.025, 16.619 and 18.853. The obtained 't' value between the two groups on achievement orientation, cognitive stimulation, recreational orientation, home structure and language stimulation is 1.8649, 0.7666, 1.0879, 2.0399 and 1.9886 respectively. 't' values obtained for achievement orientation, home structure and language stimulation are found to be significant at 0.05 level. Thus it can be said that the two groups differ significantly in their school performance on achievement orientation, home structure and language stimulation. Mean school performance score of enriched group on achievement orientation, home structure and language stimulation is higher than that of their moderate group. The scores indicate that children of moderate intelligence experiencing enriched environment on achievement orientation, home structure and language stimulation, are found to have higher school performance than those experiencing moderate environment on the same dimension.

Table -4.39 further shows that the mean school performance scores of moderate group on achievement orientation, cognitive stimulation, recreational orientation, home structure and language stimulation is 74.176, 78.071, 76.150, 71.308 and 73.846 respectively with their SDs 17.551, 18.699, 18.025, 16.619 and 18.853 (Similarly) and that low group on achievement orientation, cognitive stimulation, recreational orientation, home structure and language stimulation 60.300, 63.268, 68.077, 66.750 and 65.882 respectively with their SDs 6.278, 11.022, 16.932, 16.391 and14.311. The obtained 't' value between the two groups on achievement orientation, cognitive stimulation, recreational orientation, home structure and language stimulation is 2.9544, 2.5488, 1.2990, 0.6896 and 1.2698 respectively and the t ratios obtained for achievement orientation, cognitive stimulation only, are found to be significant at 0.05 and 0.01 level respectively. Thus it can be inferred that the two groups differ significantly in their school performance on achievement orientation and cognitive stimulation. Mean school performance scores of moderate groups on achievement orientation, and cognitive stimulation is higher than that of their low groups. The scores indicate that children of moderate intelligence experiencing moderate environment on achievement orientation, cognitive stimulation, are found to have higher school performance than those experiencing low environmnet on the same dimensions.

Results reveal that the mean school performance score of children of moderate intelligence group, experiencing enriched family environment is higher than that of those experiencing low family environment on all the five dimensions. Mean school performance score of those experiencing enriched environment on achievement orientation, home structure and language stimulation is higher than those experiencing moderate family environment on the same and that of those experiencing moderate family environment on achievement orientation and cognitive stimulation is higher than that of those experiencing lower family environment on the same.

Results indicate that children belonging to moderate intelligence group exhibit higher school performance on experiencing enriched family environment with respect to all the five dimensions of family environment, i.e., achievement orientation, cognitive stimulation, recreational orientation, home structure and language stimulation than low family environment with respect to these dimensions.

Results also indicate that children experiencing enriched family environment on achievement orientation, home structure and language stimulation exhibit higher school performance than those experiencing moderate family environment on the same.

Further results also indicate that in case of achievement orientation and cognitive stimulation, children experiencing moderate family environment exhibit better school performance than those experiencing low family environment.

Table – 4.41 shows that the mean school performance scores of enriched groups on achievement orientation, cognitive stimulation, recreational orientation, home structure and language stimulation is 80.706, 80.850, 81.053, 80.478, and 79.500 respectively with their SDs 10.582, 11.581, 11.009, 12.378, and 11.805, and that of low group on achievement orientation, cognitive stimulation, recreational orientation, home structure

Table 4.41

Significance of Difference in Mean School Performance Scores of Elementary School Children Belonging to Low Intelligence Group at Different Levels of Five Dimensions of Family Environment viz. Achievement Orientation; Cognitive Stimulation; Recreational Orientation; Home Structure; and Language Stimulation (As Perceived by Parents)

Dimensions Of Family Environment	*Family Environment Groups*	*N*	*Mean*	*SD*	*'t' ratios*	*Level of Significance*
Achievement orientation	Enriched	17	80.706	10.582		
	Vs				3.9085	0.01
	Low	25	65.400	14.789		
Cognitive stimulation	Enriched	20	80.850	11.581		
	Vs				4.9515	0.01
	Low	24	62.542	12.929		
Recreational orientation	Enriched	19	81.053	11.009		
	Vs				5.0252	0.01
	Low	22	62.500	12.630		
Home structure	Enriched	23	80.478	12.378		
	Vs				4.7206	0.01
	Low	25	63.760	12.120		
Language stimulation	Enriched	18	79.500	11.815		
	Vs				4.7327	0.01
	Low	21	61.714	11.564		
Achievement	Enriched	17	80.706	10.582		

(contd.)

Contd.

Dimensions of Family Environment	*Family Environment Groups*	*N*	*Mean*	*SD*	*'t' ratios*	*Level of Significance*
orientation	Vs				2.4021	0.05
	Moderate	17	71.353	12.073		
Cognitive	Enriched	20	80.850	11.581		
stimulation	Vs				1.9271	0.05
	Moderate	15	73.467	10.935		
Recreational	Enriched	19	81.053	11.009		
orientation	Vs				2.1900	0.05
	Moderate	18	72.500	12.637		
Home	Enriched	23	80.478	12.378		
structure	Vs				2.2200	0.05
	Moderate	11	70.455	12.287		
Language	Enriched	18	79.500	11.815		
stimulation	Vs				1.1903	NS
	Moderate	20	74.650	13.301		
Achievement	Moderate	17	71.353	12.078		
orientation	Vs				1.4303	NS
	Low	25	65.400	14.789		
Cognitive	Moderate	15	73.467	10.935		
stimulation	Vs				2.8267	0.01
	Low	24	62.542	12.929		
Recreational	Moderate	18	72.500	12.637		
orientation	Vs				2.4904	0.05
	Low	22	62.500	12.630		
Home	Moderate	11	70.455	12.287		
structure	Vs				1.5121	NS
	Low	25	63.760	12.120		
Language	Moderate	20	74.650	13.301		
stimulation	Vs				3.3164	0.01
	Low	21	61.714	11.564		

and language stimulation is 65.400, 62.542, 62.500, 63.760 and 61.714 respectively with their SDs 14.789, 12.929, 12.630, 12.120 and 11.564. The obtained 't' value between the two groups on achievement orientation, cognitive stimulation, recreational orientation, home structure and language stimulation is 3.9085, 4.9515, 5.0252, 4.7216, and 4.7327 respectively and all of these are found to be significant at .01 level. Thus it can be inferred that the two groups differ significantly in their school performance. Mean school performance score of enriched group on all the five dimensions viz. achievement orientation, cognitive stimulation, recreational orientation, home structure and language stimulation is higher than that of their low group. The scores indicate that children of low intelligence group experiencing enriched environment on achievement orientation, cognitive stimulation, recreational orientation, home structure and language stimulation, are found to have higher school performance than those experiencing low environment on the same dimensions.

Table – 4.41 also shows that the mean school performance score of enriched groups on achievement orientation, cognitive stimulation, recreational orientation, home structure and language stimulation is 80.706, 80.850, 81.053, 80.478 and 79.500 respectively with their SDs 10.582, 11.581, 11.009, 12.378, and 11.805, and that of moderate group on achievement orientation, cognitive stimulation, recreational orientation, home structure and language stimulation is 71.35373.467, 72.500, 70.455 and 74.650 respectively with their SDs 12.078, 10.935, 12.637, 12.287 and 13.301. The obtained 't' value between the two groups on achievement orientation, cognitive stimulation, recreational orientation, home structure and language stimulation is 2.4021, 1.9271, 2.1900, 2.2200 and 1.1903 and these are found to be significant for achievement orientation, cognitive stimulation, recreational orientation and home structure at 0.05 level except for recreational orientation, which is significant at 0.05 level. Thus it can be said that the two groups differ significantly in their school performance achievement orientation, cognitive stimulation, recreational orientation and home structure. Mean school performance score of enriched group on achievement orientation, cognitive stimulation, recreational orientation and home structure is higher than that of their moderate group. The scores indicate that children belonging to Enriched group of achievement orientation, cognitive stimulation, recreational orientation and home structure, are found to have higher school performance than those belonging to Moderate group of the same dimension.

Table –4.41 further shows that the mean school performance scores of moderate group on achievement orientation, cognitive stimulation, recreational orientation, home structure and language stimulation is 71.353, 73.467, 72.500, 70.455 and 74.650 respectively with their SDs 12.078, 10.935,

12.637, 12.287 and 13.301. and that low group on achievement orientation, cognitive stimulation, recreational orientation, home structure and language stimulation is 65.400, 62.542, 62.500, 63.760 and 61.714 respectively with their SDs 14.789, 12.929, 12.630, 12.120 and 11.564. The obtained 't' value between the two groups on achievement orientation, cognitive stimulation, recreational orientation, home structure and language stimulation is 1.4303, 2.8267, 2.4904, 1.5121 and 3.3164 respectively and the t. ratios obtained for achievement orientation and language stimulation, only, are found to be significant at 0.05 and 0.01 level respectively. Thus it can be inferred that the two groups differ significantly in their school performance on achievement orientation and language stimulation. Mean school performance scores of moderate groups on achievement orientation, and language stimulation is higher than that of their low groups. The scores indicate that children of low intelligence group experiencing moderate environment on achievement orientation, language stimulation, are found to have higher school performance than those experiencing low environment on the same dimensions.

Thus results indicate that children belonging to low intelligence group exhibit better school performance on experiencing enriched family environment with respect to all the five dimensions of family environment i.e., achievement orientation, cognitive stimulation, recreational orientation, home structure and language stimulation than those experiencing low family environment with respect to these dimensions.

Results also indicate that children experiencing enriched family environment on achievement orientation, cognitive stimulation, recreational orientation and home structure exhibit better school performance than those experiencing moderate family environment on the same.

Further results also indicate that in case of cognitive stimulation, recreational orientation and language stimulation, children experiencing moderate family environment exhibit better school performance than those experiencing low family environment.

For a clear comprehension of results comparisons of 't' ratios and mean school performance scores of table 4.39, 4.40 and 4.41 are presented in table 4.42 and 4.43 respectively.

Table 4.42

Comparisons of 't' Ratios Obtained for School Performance Differentials of Elementary School Children Belonging to Similar Intelligence Groups viz. High, Moderate and Low, at Different Levels of Family Environment i.e., Enriched, Moderate and Low with Respect to all the Five Dimension of Family Environment. (as percent by parents)

Intelligence →		*High Intelligence*	*Moderate Intelligence*	*Low Intelligence*
Dimension ofF.E.	*Level ofF.E.*			
	En vs Lo	2.2567 *	6.6126 **	3.9085 **
AO	En vs Mo	2.3281 **	1.8649 *	2.4021 *
	Mo vs Lo	0.5385	2.9544**	1.4303
	En vs Lo	2.5517 **	4.5763 **	4.9515 **
CS	En vs Mo	1.2870	0.7666	1.9271 *
	Mo vs Lo	1.1587	2.5488 **	2.8267 **
	En vs Lo	2.1679 *	2.4299 *	5.0252 **
RO	En vs Mo	0.0930	1.0879	2.1900 *
	Mo vs Lo	1.7416 *	1.2990	2.4904 *
	En vs Lo	2.0700*	2.9732* *	4.7216 **
HS	En vs Mo	0.1369	2.0399*	2.2200 *
	Mo vs Lo	1.7186	0.6896	1.5121
	En vs Lo	1.8953 *	4.5097 **	4.7327 **
LS	En vs Mo	0.5402	1.9886 *	1.1903
	Mo vs Lo	1.1.359	1.2698	3.3164 **

** significant at 0.01 level; * significant at 0.05 level

F.E- Family Environment; AO = Achievement Oriented

CS = Cognitive Stimulation; RO = Recreational Orientation

HS = Home Structure; LS = Language Stimulation,

En = Enriched; Mo = Moderate; Lo = Low

Table 4.43
Comparison of Mean School Performance Scores of Elementary School Children Belonging to Similar Intelligence Group viz. High, Moderate and Low, and Experiencing Different Family Environment i.e., Enriched, Moderate and Low with Respect to Five Dimension of Family Environment (as perceived by parents).

Intelligence →		*High Intelligence*	*Moderate Intelligence*	*Low Intelligence*
Dimension of F.E.	*Level of F.E.*			
	Enriched	91.059	83.840	80.706
AO	Moderate	82.154	74.176	71.353
	Low	78.882	60.300	65.400
	Enriched	90.621	82.542	80.850
CS	Moderate	85.563	78.071	73.463
	Low	79.368	63.286	62:542
	Enriched	88.969	81.684	81.053
RO	Moderate	88.583	76.150	72.500
	Low	79.750	68.077	62.500
	Enriched	87.400	82.667	80.478
HS	Moderate	87.083	71.308	70.455
	Low	78.083	66.750	63.760
	Enriched	86.524	85.445	79.500
LS	Moderate	83.941	73.846	74.650
	Low	78.452	65.882	61.714

F.E. = Family Environment; AO = Achievement Orientation
CS = Cognitive Stimulation; RO = Recreated Orientation
HS = Home Structure; LS = Language Stimulation

Tables 4.42 indicates that significant differences in the mean school performance score of elementary school children at different levels of their family environment (as perceived by Parents) are to be seen in the case of *Enriched – Low* family environment groups of children belonging to all the three groups of intelligence i.e. *High, Moderate, and Low intelligence groups,* with respect to all the five dimensions viz. Achievement orientation, Cognitive stimulation, Recreational orientation, Home structure and Language stimulation. Such differences are also found between Moderate – Low family environment group of children on

Recreational orientation and language stimulation in case of high intelligence group; on Achievement orientation and Cognitive stimulation in case of moderate family environment group of children and on Cognitive stimulation, Recreational orientation, and Language stimulation in case of low intelligence group of children.

It can be observed from table 4.43 that mean school performance scores of enriched family environment group of children are higher than that of low family environment group of children belonging to all the three groups of intelligence, i.e., high, moderate and low intelligence groups on Achievement orientation, Cognitive stimulation, Recreational orientation, Home structure and Language stimulation. Also mean school performance scores of enriched family environment group are higher than that of moderate family environment group of children on achievement orientation in case of high intelligence; on achievement orientation, home structure and language stimulation in case of moderate intelligence group; on achievement orientation, Cognitive stimulation, Recreational orientation, Home structure. In addition to the it also found that mean school performance of moderate family environment group of children is higher than that of low intelligence group of children on Cognitive stimulation, Recreational orientation and Language stimulation.

Therefore Hy 8 of the present study that ' if a child experiences better family environment (school focussed parent child interaction), *as perceived by Parents*, then a child will have higher school performance, than a child with *similar intelligence,* experiencing not so good family environment' is retained at :

(i) *Enriched – Low* level for children of all the three groups of intelligence i.e. *High, Moderate; and Low intelligence* on all the five dimensions viz achievement orientation , cognitive stimulation, recreational orientation, home structure and language stimulation.

(ii) *Enriched - Moderate* level for children of *high intelligence group* on achievement orientation; for children of *moderate intelligence group* on achievement orientation, home structure and language stimulation; and for children of *low intelligence group* on achievement orientation, cognitive stimulation, recreational orientation and home structure.

(iii) *Moderate – Low* level for children of *high intelligence group* on recreational orientation and home structure, for children of *moderate intelligence group* on achievement orientation and cognitive stimulation, and for children of *low intelligence group* on cognitive stimulation , recreational orientation and language stimulation.

Discussion of Results

In this section an attempt is made to discuss the results obtained. School performance of elementary school children in relation to there Family Environment, Intelligence, and Socio-economic status as brought out in terms of correlates; School Performance differentials at different levels of Family Environment and School Performance differentials of elementary school children belonging to similar intelligence groups at different levels of family environment have already been presented in sections 4.1, 4.2 and 4.3 respectively in this chapter.

Findings of the present study report a significant positive relationship of school performance with family environment and its five dimensions viz. Achievement orientation, cognitive stimulation, recreational orientation, home structure. (as perceived by children and parents)

Results also suggest that children belonging to families having enriched family environment (on all the five dimensions) are found to have better school performance in comparison to children coming from families having moderate family environment and low family environment. (as perceived by children and parents)

However there is no significant difference in the mean scores of school performance in case of comparison between moderate and low family environment in case of overall family environment, achievement orientation, and recreational orientation as perceived by children and in the case of achievement orientation, recreational orientation, and home structure as perceived by parents.

In an analysis of school performance of children having similar intelligence at different level of family environment, indicate that children coming from families having enriched environment are found to have better school performance in comparison to children coming from moderate and low family environment.

In order to evaluate the obtained results against other studies conducted on similar or comparable variables, a review of literature revealed an extreme scarcity of such studies, particularly on the Impact of Family Environment (School focussed parent child interaction) on school performance of elementary school children.

One of the most relevant research efforts, by Muralidharan (1990), seems to be very appropriate for the comparison of findings with those of the present study.

Muralidharan (1990) in an article based on the an empirical project entitled 'The kind of environmental variable that affect the achievement of children in primary schools' (NCERT 1970-1974) writes about the study that investigated the effect of Parent related, School related, Child centered variables, socio-economic status and facilities provided at home on the achievement of children in primary schools.

The sample consisted of 664 children belonging to classes I, II, and V in the age group of 5 to 11 years was studied. First order correlation were worked out between independent variables and dependent variables and also between intervening variables.

The findings showed that almost all home variables – maternal behaviour, attitudes as well as facilities- have a significant relationship with the child's achievement in school in contrast the school variables did not prove to have much effect on the child's achievement. The socio-economic variable proved to be consistently having a significant impact. Amongst the child related variables, the child's independence was found to effect his achievement. Ethical discriminations as well as positive concept have an effect on the school achievement in the case of younger children.

Findings also highlight that ultimately it is the home variables and the child's intelligence which would account for differences in the school achievement of children.

Results of the core study of this project (NCERT 1978) revealed that Home environment and children's intelligence account for differences in academic achievement; moreover keeping IQ and SES constant, the single most important factor that tilted the balance in favour of school achievement was the facilitation language development in the home.

On comparing the findings of the present investigations with the above mentioned study, it is observed that family environment is a vital factor in the school performance of school children.

Another research study conducted by Mishra and Tiwari (1990) to understand cognitive development of children from an ecological perspective seems to be within the same frame of reference as used in the present study. Therefore, they provide useful findings for the purpose of comparison with the present investigation. They conducted a study by taking a sample of 300 children (180 boys and 120 girls) and their families. Children were drawn from III, IV and V classes of inferior and superior schools located in rural and urban setting of Uttar Pradesh.

A comprehensive measure of objective and perceived environment dealing with proximal environmental variable developed by the authors was used to assess the environmental characteristics. The other tools used were RPM/DAT/ Bender-Gestalt test and story, pictorial embedded figure test.

The findings suggest that environmental influences are multifaceted and depend upon the specific nature of cognitive skills as well as the developmental stage of children. The findings of the present investigation seem to be quite in agreement with those mentioned in the study to the extent that family environment is multifaceted in nature and as such school focus parent child interaction (family environment) have an effect on school performance of children.

Similar trends are also available in the western context. Working with a sample of white fifth grade American children, both Dave (1963) and Wolf (1964) found that their measure of environment accounted for approximately 50 per cent of the variance in the global intelligence test score . Dyer (1967), who examined fifth grade West Indian children, found that environmental score accounted for 46 per cent of the variance in global intelligence test scores. Marjoribanks (1972) working with 11years old boys and their parents found that 52 per cent of the variance in global intelligence test score could be attributed to the measured environmental forces. These research efforts have shown that the environmental forces do have a direct bearing on the school performance of children.

The findings of similar studies like Karnes (1972), Rohwer (1970), Kellaghan (1977), Ausbel, Sullivan and Ives (1980), Scott Jones (1984), Stevenson and Baker (1987), McCartney and Mouley (1992) also indicate that cognitive benefits of environmental enrichment are well established.

Inborn ability or intelligence is another factor that influences the school performance of the child. Findings of the present study also point out towards a similar relationship. These results draw strength from similar study (Muralidharan, 1990) which concluded that ultimately the home variables and the intelligence of the child that account for differences in the school achievement of children.

Rao (1977) writing on 'Concept development in children', noted that on the Piagetian task of conservation, the effect of socio-economic status was negligible until the age of 5½ years. Beyond that age there was significant difference between high and low socio-economic status children, which increased with age.

Results of the present study suggest that SES and school performance of a child are not related to each other. (However) some studies report a significant relationship of SES with a child's school achievement. (Muralidharan 1990), (White 1982). While Bradley, Caldwel and Elardo (1977) in an investigation to compare environmental process measure and SES measure in terms of their relation with standford- Binet IQ at 3 years of age found that , process measure appear to be more accurate index of environmental quality across groups than SES. Similarly Marjoribanks (1972) in a study also pointed at that environmental measure accounted for more of the variance in the ability scores than did a set of social status indicators.

5
Main Findings, Educational Implication and Suggestion for Further Research

On the strength of the analysis, interpretation and discussion of results, the investigator is in a position to draw main findings. This chapter deals with the main findings, educational implications and suggestions for further research, that are presented in the same sequence.

Main Findings

As is evident from chapter –I, the present study is aimed at investigating the ' Impact of family environment on the School performance of elementary school children.' The data collected for this purpose was subjected to statistical analysis in three sections to reach at main findings. For a clear comprehension a section wise presentation of findings is made.

Section 5.1.1 deals with findings obtained on the basis of correlation between school performance of elementary school children and their family environment (as perceived by Children and Parents) and also between school performance and their intelligence and socio economic status.

Section 5.1.2 presents the findings with respect to the impact of family environment on school performance of elementary school children as brought out by school performance differentials at different levels of family environment (as perceived by children and parents).

Section 5.1.3 deals with findings arrived at after isolating the influence of intelligence on school performance, in terms of school performance differentials of children belonging to similar intelligence groups, at different levels of family environment. (as perceived by children and parents).

School Performance of Elementary School Children in Relation to their Family Environment, Intelligence and Socio-Economic Status

1. School performance of elementary school children has been found to have significant and positive relationship with *Children's Perception* of *Overall Family Environment* and its five dimensions viz. *Achievement orientation, Cognitive stimulation, Recreational orientation, Home structure, and Language stimulation.* It was also found that language stimulation has relatively higher relationship with school performance in comparison to other dimensions of family environment.
2. School performance of elementary school children is found to have significant and positive relationship with *Parent's Perception* of *Overall Family Environment*, and its five dimensions viz. *Achievement orientation, Cognitive stimulation, Recreational orientation, Home structure, and Language stimulation.* It was also found that achievement orientation and cognitive stimulation dimensions of family environment, have relatively higher relationship with school performance in comparison to other dimensions.
3. School performance of elementary school children has been found to have significant and positive relationship with their *intelligence*.
4. School performance of elementary school children is not found to have significant relationship with their *socio economic status.*

Impact of Family Environment on School Performance of Elementary School Children as Brought out by School Performance Differentials at Different Levels of Family Environment

1. Children experiencing *Enriched Family Environment* (*as perceived by Children)* are found to exhibit higher school performance than those, experiencing either *Moderate or Low Family Environment.* And also children experiencing Moderate Family Environment are found to exhibit higher school performance than those experiencing *Low Family Environment*, both in terms of *Overall family environment* as well as its five dimensions viz. *Achievement orientation, Cognitive stimulation, Recreational orientation, Home structure, and Language stimulation as perceived by Children*.
2. Children experiencing *Enriched Family Environment* (*as perceived Parents)* are found to exhibit higher school performance in comparison to those children who experience *Moderate and Low*

Family Environment in terms of both *Overall family environment* as well as its five dimensions viz. *Achievement orientation, Cognitive stimulation, Recreational orientation, Home structure, and Language Stimulation*

And children experiencing *Moderate Family Environment* show higher school performance in comparison to the children who experience *Low family environment* in terms of *Overall family environment, Cognitive stimulation and Recreational orientation as perceived by Parents.*

Impact of Family Environment on School Performance of Elementary School Children Belonging to Similar Intelligence Groups as Brought out by School Performance Differentials at Different Levels of Family Environment (As Perceived by Children and Parents)

After isolating the influence of intelligence on school performance of elementary school children it is found that:-

1. Children belonging to all the three groups of similar intelligence i.e. *high, moderate and low intelligence groups* exhibit higher school performance on experiencing *Enriched Family Environment* than those children who experience either *Moderate or Low Family Environment* in terms of *Overall family environment.* Where as no significant differences are found between *Moderate-Low Family Environment groups* with respect to *Overall family environment (as perceived by children).*
2. Children belonging to all the three groups of similar intelligence i.e. *high, moderate and low intelligence groups* exhibit higher school performance on experiencing *Enriched Family Environment* with respect to all the five dimensions of family environment viz. *Achievement orientation, Cognitive stimulation, Recreational orientation, Home structure, and Language stimulation,* than those experiencing *Low Family Environment* with respect to these five dimensions *(as perceived by children).*

Such differences are also found between *Enriched- Moderate Family Environment* group on *Recreational orientation* for *high intelligence group* of children; on *Home structure* for *moderate intelligence group* of children; and on *all the five dimensions* for *low intelligence group* of children.

In case of *Moderate – Low Family Environment* groups no such difference are found for any of the five dimensions in case of all the three groups of intelligence.

3. Children belonging all the three groups of similar intelligence i.e. *high, moderate and low intelligence groups* exhibit higher school

performance on experiencing *Enriched Family Environment* than those children who experience *Low Family Environment* with respect to *Overall family environment.* In addition to this, in case of *low intelligence group* of children, it is found that children experiencing *Enriched Family Environment* exhibit higher school performance than those who experience *Moderate Family Environment* and for same group such differences are also found between *Moderate – Low Family Environment* group with respect to *Overall family environment (as perceived by Parents).*

4. Children having similar intelligence *i.e high, moderate and low* exhibit higher school performance on experiencing *Enriched Family Esnvironment* with respect to all the five dimensions of family environment viz. *Achievement orientation, Cognitive stimulation, Recreational orientation, Home structure, and Language stimulation,* than those experiencing *Low family environment* with respect to these five dimensions (as perceived by Parents)

Such differences are also found between *Enriched–Moderate Family Environment* group on *Achievement orientation* for children *high intelligence group*; on *Achievement orientation, Home structure and Language stimulation* for children of *moderate intelligence group* and on *Achievement orientation, Cognitive stimulation, Recreational orientation and Home structure* for children of *low intelligence group.*

Differences like these are also found between *Moderate-Low family environment group* on *recreational orientation and home structure* for children of *high intelligence group*; on *achievement orientation and cognitive stimulation* for children of *moderate intelligence group* and on *cognitive stimulation recreational orientation and language stimulation* for *low intelligence group* of children.

Educational Implication

In the light of findings of the study there is a need to organize intervention programmes for Parents, Teachers, and Students/ Children.

Intervention programs for parents should aim at the enrichment of the family environment, so as to enable the parents to contribute better in the School performance of children. These intervention programmes for parents can be of two types Individualized and Group intervention programmes. Such programs may be organized through schools where not only awareness and orientation be provided to parents but also adequate training concerning ways and means through which Enriched school focussed interactions be achieved.

In addition to this, separate orientation programmes be also conducted for Teachers so as to enable then to compensate children with the very absence or inadequacies existing in families with Moderate and Low family environment.

Efforts are equally needed to help teachers play their role as to benefit the parents in general and especially those belonging to moderate and Low family environment.

The educational institutions like school can screen homes to identify those posing a risk to the child's School performance, by not providing the needed stimulation and support.

Further, governmental as well as non-governmental efforts are required in order to establish Resource Centers facilitating School and Parental efforts aimed at providing a better family environment to the child. Such centers must try to cater to the needs of Parents, Teachers and the Children. Their function may include providing quality of activities that involve the family in the usage of language Computation skills and Problem solving as well as Parental reinforcement of child's behaviour established in the school.

Educational institutions like Universities, NCERT, NIEPA, etc. can help in the development of resource materials suited to the needs of Resource centers.

In the present study it has been found that home environment does play a very vital role in the performance of the child at school and improvements are needed in low family environments. With this point of view the present study underlines that it is very important that society develops national policies and programmes to ensure that families are able to provide their children with an environment conducive to success in later life. Hence, policies can be worked out to provide the resources and nurturences that young children need to function as effective members of modern society.

Suggestion for Further Research

Generally one of the outcomes of conducting any research study is to generate avenues for further research. The present study entitled 'Impact of family environment on School performance of elementary school children, also points to the same directions, the related research workers may choose to opt for in the near future.

The results of the present study throw a valuable light on the usefulness of School –focussed parent child interactions on the school performance of elementary school children. But the present study is based on a sample drawn from a limited geographical area and is confined to class V students only. It would be appreciable if similar research efforts are put in with a sample drawn from wider geographical area and having a variety of subjects for further research studies.

Results of the present study indicate the importance of family environment on the school performance of elementary school children. However, taking into consideration the difference in parent – child interactions at different stages of development, similar studies may be conducted for Pre-school and secondary school students also.

Comparative studies covering different levels of education, i.e., pre-primary, primary, elementary, and secondary stages be also conducted to find out the impact of family environment on performance of student belonging to different age- groups.

Studies to develop resource material and design intervention strategies for the needy parents may also be carried out.

Evaluative studies may also be taken up to go into the effect of intervention strategies designed for the needy parents.

The present study was limited to similar school environment. Similar effort can be put in to conduct studies on different type of school environmental like Rural – Urban, Govt. – Private, Aided – Unaided.

Effect of school focussed interactions provided by different members in the family can also be studied.

Comprehensive studies of family environment characteristics covering Psycho – social characteristics as well as status characteristics, as associated with school performance of children may also be carried out.

Summary

Introduction

Each child is unique. This is obvious and astonishing and we do well to remember it whenever we start to speak of children, school and, education. The individual child is after all what the whole process of education is centered around. If we start from an individual child most of us can quickly say what we most want for him-that he should grow and develop physically, emotionally and mentally so that he becomes an independent adult, the master and not the slave of circumstances. Mostly, it is education that helps him to do this.

Educational theories reveal that there is a general acceptance of significance of childhood experiences in the later educational growth of a person. Therefore a striking feature of contemporary educational thinking has been a growing concern about the effectiveness and efficiency of teaching learning outcomes of a system of education with regard to Family Environment.

Viewing education as a means of development obviously means that we need to evolve certain educational models with the help of which changes in the form of educational growth can be brought about. Individual differences due to genetic potential of the child are beyond the control of growth scientists and educationists. But identification of environmental factors favourable for educational growth can help in creating those wholesome experiences.

Two institutions that impinge most directly on the nature and quality of child's educational experiences and development are 'the family' and 'the school'. It is a common and plausible assumption that families prepare and reinforce the symbolic attribution required by schooling and that schooling builds upon and elaborates the symbolic resources derived from family membership.

Justification of the Study

School performance is not an independent phenomenon, rather it is directly influenced by a number of factors, some of which are personal to the individual while many others are located in the environment in which the learning takes place i.e. school and family. Early beginnings to knowledge originate within the family, on a simple level in early years, and are then further built on in the school. Family sets the stage for interactions and learning at school later.

Families vary greatly in structure and functioning. Variations exist also in school and in children themselves. Given this diversity in families, there is a need to understand how children's experiences within the family contribute to their educational outcomes.

The family context often has been conceptualized as status variable such as socio-economic status. Research evidence indicates that socio-economic status is positively correlated with school performance but is not very significant. Broad static measures of SES typically are used, without a detailed examination of behavior and experiences that may differ or remain constant across socio-economic level.

Societal changes brought about as a result of technological advancement have had a dramatic impact on family environment in both developing and developed countries. This in turn has brought about a radical change in roles of different family members and parent-child interactions. A consensus is building, however that status variables are not as important as are family process variables in predicting academic success.

Since few researches in India have attempted to focus on the influence of changing family environment, there is need to study how different family process variables like cognitive stimulation, achievement orientation, recreational orientation, home structure and language stimulation, relate to School performance of Indian children.

Developmental psychologists have highlighted the importance of developmental status of the child. During the early formative years the child has two worlds-'Family and School'. Family environment influences individual differently according to the child's age. Variable affecting a six-year-old child may not necessarily operate in the same manner after the child has been in the school for several more years. Moreover as the child grows older and moves from being dependent on others to being independent, there is a decline in parent-child interaction. Thus, there is need to develop better insight into the influence of family environment on school performance of elementary school children as during this period the child is likely to interact more with his parents and other family members.

Since the acceptance of education as a constitutional right of children in the age group of 6-14 years, elementary education has been an area of concern for both, the educationist and the government of India. National Policy of Education –1986, has underlined the importance of elementary education with attention being focussed on Universalzation of elementary Education. Though the figures of enrolment have risen consistently, we still have a sizeable number of children outside the school stream. Universal enrolment is indeed a difficult problem, but even more so is the universal retention. Hence, there arises the need to study the influence of family environment on elementary school children as various advantageous and disadvantageous environments in the family and school influence the nature and quality of child's educational experiences. Therefore, no matter what we do inside the school, we can not make a significant impact without the informed support of the family.

Further the need of the study can be justified on the basis of findings of Balesky (1990) that parents rearing their children in a climate of affection and responsiveness, using clear and explicable rules, providing developmentally enhancing and autonomy granting environment, are more likely to have children with positive self concept who are emotionally stable, socially competent, well accepted by their peers, academically successful and intrinsically self responsible.

Thus research studies provided in the background do attach importance to the significance of family process variable on school performance. However in the Indian social-cultural context enough evidence regarding the relationship between family environment and school performance, is lacking to make some genralizations. The investigation of such relationship is typically missing at the elementary level of education, which is considered to be a foundation period. Therefore, study of family environment, as affecting the school performance of elementary school children seems fully justified. It is in this background that the present study is undertaken, more specifically the following is the problem undertaken

Statement of the Problem

"Impact of Family Environment on School Performance of Elementary School Children"

Operational Definition of the Terms Used

School Performance

School performance refers to scholastic attainment of the child in different subjects as an indicator of cognitive and intellectual skills acquired during the course of teaching learning process. For the purpose of present study marks obtained in class V are considered as school performance.

Family Environment

For the present investigation family environment refers to school focussed Parent Child interactions with regard to cognitive stimulation, achievement orientation, recreational orientation, home structure and language development.

Objectives of the Study

(I) To develop and standardize a scale for measuring family environment.

(II) To study the relationship of School Performance of elementary school children with Family Environment and its dimension as perceived by Children.

(III) To study the relationship of School Performance of elementary school children with Family Environment and its dimension as perceived by Parents.

(IV) To study the relationship between school performance and intelligence.

(V) To study the relationship between school performance and socio economic status.

(VI) To study the impact of family environment on school performance of elementary school children as brought out by school performance differentials at different levels of their Family Environment *as perceived by children.*

(VII) To study the impact of family environment on school performance of elementary school children as brought out by school performance differentials at different levels of their Family Environment *as perceived by Parents.*

(VIII) To study the impact of family environment on school performance of elementary school children, after isolating the influence of intelligence on their school performance, in terms of school performance differentials at differentials at different levels of their family environments and its dimension *as perceived by Children.*

(IX) To study the impact of family environment on school performance of elementary school children, after isolating the influence of intelligence on their school performance, in terms of school performance differentials at differentials at different levels of their family environments and its dimension *as perceived by Parents.*

Hypotheses

I. There exists a significant positive relationship between School Performance of elementary school children and Family Environment *as perceived by Children.*

II. There exists a significant positive relationship between School Performance of elementary school children and Family Environment *as perceived by Parents.*

III. There exists a significant positive relationship between School Performance of elementary school children and their Intelligence..

IV. There exists a significant positive relationship between School Performance of elementary school children and their Socio-economic status.

V. If chilu experiences better family environment (school focused parent child interactions), then the child will exhibit higher school performance than the one, who experiences not so good family environment *as perceived by Children.*

VI. If child experiences better family environment (school focused parent child interactions), then the child will exhibit higher school performance than the one, who experiences not so good family environment *as perceived by Parents.*

VII. If child experiences better family environment (school focused parent child interactions), then the child will exhibit higher school performance than the one, *with similar intelligence,* who experiences not so good family environment *as perceived by Children.*

VIII. If child experiences better family environment (school focused parent child interactions), then the child will exhibit higher school performance than the one, *with similar intelligence,* who experiences not so good family environment *as perceived by Parents.*

Delimitation of the Study

The present study is presented within the following confinements:

The study is limited to class V students of D.A.V. Centenary Public Schools of Haryana.

The study is conducted only in the three districts of Haryana viz. Ambala, Karnal, and Kurukshetra.

The sample of the study is confined to all the class V students of four D.A.V. Centenary Public Schools selected randomly and their parents.

In the presented study Family Environment is delimited to five dimensions viz. Achievement Orientation, Cognitive Stimulation, Recreational Orientation, Home Structure and Language Stimulation.

Method

Keeping in view the nature of the present study, researcher has used survey method to describe and interpret what exists at present in terms of relationship and differences between school performance of elementary school children and their family environment as perceived by *children* and *parents.*

Sample

The present study aims at investigating the impact of family environment on school performance of elementary school children. Keeping in view the delimitation of the study, population of the present study consisted of class V student of DAV Public Schools of Haryana and their Parents.

Three districts namely Ambala, Karnal and Kurukshetra out of the nineteen districts of Haryana were purposively selected. Four DAV Centenary Public Schools, managed by DAV College managing committee, Chitragupt Road, New Delhi, were selected randomly. Selection of these schools of similar nature, run by DAV management was guided by some important considerations like uniformity of policies, programmes and standards of evaluation followed by these institutions under the same management. All the students of class V of these four school selected randomly, present on the day in their respective schools and their parents were taken as sample.

Tools Used

The following tools were used for collecting the required data.

- Family environment scale for Children developed and standardized by the researcher.
- Family Environment Scale for Parents - developed and standardized by the researcher.
- Non Verbal Intelligence test developed by Navodaya Vidayalya Samiti and adapted by the researcher.
- Socio Economic Status Inventory prepared by the researcher.

Statistical Techniques Used

The data was analyzed with the help of following statistical techniques:

1. Co-efficient of correlation to find out the relationship.
2. t-ratio to find out the differentials.

Main Findings

1. School performance of elementary school children has been found to have significant and positive relationship with *Children's Perception* of *Overall Family Environment* and its five dimensions viz. *Achievement orientation, Cognitive stimulation, Recreational orientation, Home structure, and Language stimulation.* It was also found that language stimulation has relatively higher relationship with school performance in comparison to other dimensions of family environment.
2. School performance of elementary school children is found to have significant and positive relationship with *Parent's Perception* of *Overall Family Environment,* and its five dimensions viz. *Achievement orientation, Cognitive stimulation, Recreational orientation, Home structure, and Language stimulation.* It was also found that achievement orientation and cognitive stimulation dimensions of family environment ,have relatively higher relationship with school performance in comparison to other dimensions.
3. School performance of elementary school children has been found to have significant and positive relationship with their *intelligence.*
4. School performance of elementary school children is not found to have significant relationship with their *socio economic status.*
5. Children experiencing *Enriched Family Environment* (*as perceived by Children)* are found to exhibit higher school performance than those, experiencing either *Moderate or Low Family Environment.* And also children experiencing Moderate Family Environment are found to exhibit higher school performance than those experiencing *Low Family Environment,* both in terms of *Overall family environment* as well as its five dimensions viz. *Achievement orientation, Cognitive stimulation, Recreational orientation, Home structure, and Language stimulation as perceived by Children.*
6. Children experiencing *Enriched Family Environment as perceived Parents* are found to exhibit higher school performance in comparison to those children who experience *Moderate and Low Family Environment* in terms of both *Overall family environment* as well as its five dimensions viz. *Achievement orientation, Cognitive stimulation, Recreational orientation, Home structure, and Language stimulation.*

   And the children experiencing *Moderate Family Environment* show higher school performance in comparison to the children who experience *Low family environment* in terms of *Overall family environment, Cognitive stimulation and Recreational orientation as perceived by Parents.*

7. Children belonging to all the three groups of similar intelligence i.e. *high, moderate and low intelligence groups* exhibit higher school performance on experiencing *Enriched Family Environment* than those children who experience either *Moderate or Low Family Environment* in terms of *Overall family environment.* Where as no significant differences are found between *Moderate-Low Family Environment groups* with respect to Overall family environment *(as perceived by children).*
8. Children belonging to all the three groups of similar intelligence i.e. *high, moderate and low intelligence groups* exhibit higher school performance on experiencing *Enriched Family Environment* with respect to all the five dimensions of family environment viz. *Achievement orientation, Cognitive stimulation, Recreational orientation, Home structure, and Language stimulation,* than those experiencing *Low Family Environment* with respect to these five dimensions *(as perceived by children).*

Such differences are also found between *Enriched- Moderate Family Environment* group on *Recreational orientation* for *high intelligence group* of children; on *Home structure* for *moderate intelligence group* of children; and on *all the five dimensions* for *low intelligence group* of children.

In case of *Moderate – Low Family Environment* groups no such difference are found for any of the five dimensions in case of all the three groups of intelligence.

9. Children belonging all the three groups of similar intelligence i.e. *high, moderate and low intelligence groups* exhibit higher school performance on experiencing *Enriched Family Environment* than those children who experience *Low Family Environment* with respect to *Overall family environment.* In addition to this, in case of *low intelligence group* of children, it is found that children experiencing *Enriched Family Environment* exhibit higher school performance than those who experience *Moderate Family Environment* and for same group such differences are also found between *Moderate – Low Family Environment* group with respect to *Overall family environment (as perceived by Parents).*
10. Children having similar intelligence *i.e high, moderate and low* exhibit higher school performance on experiencing *enriched family environment* with respect to all the five dimensions of family environment viz. *Achievement orientation, Cognitive stimulation, Recreational orientation, Home structure, and Language stimulation,* than those experiencing *Low family environment* with respect to these

respect to these five dimensions (as perceived by Parents)

Such differences are also found between *Enriched–Moderate Family Environment* group on *Achievement orientation* for children *high intelligence group*; on *Achievement orientation, Home structure and Language stimulation* for children of *moderate intelligence group* and on *Achievement orientation, Cognitive stimulation, Recreational orientation and Home structure* for children of *low intelligence group.*

Differences like these are also found between *Moderate-Low family environment group* on *recreational orientation and home structure* for children of *high intelligence group*; on *achievement orientation and cognitive stimulation* for children of *moderate intelligence group* and on *cognitive stimulation recreational orientation and language stimulation* for *low intelligence group* of children.

Educational Implication

In the light of findings of the study there is a need to organize intervention programmes for Parents, Teachers, and Children.

Intervention programs for parents should aim at the enrichment of the family environment, so as to enable the parents to contribute better in the School performance of children. These intervention programmes for parents can be of two types Individualized and Group intervention programmes. Such programs may be organized through schools where not only awareness and orientation be provided to parents but also adequate training concerning ways and means through which Enriched school focussed interactions be achieved.

In addition to this, separate orientation programmes be also conducted for Teachers so as to enable then to compensate children with the very absence or inadequacies existing in families with Moderate and Low family environment.

Efforts are equally needed to help teachers play their role as to benefit the parents in general and especially those belonging to moderate and Low family environment.

The educational institutions like school can screen homes to identify those posing a risk to the child's School performance, by not providing the needed stimulation and support.

Further, governmental as well as non-governmental efforts are required in order to establish Resource Centers facilitating School and Parental efforts aimed at providing a better family environment to the child. Such centers must try to cater to the needs of Parents, Teachers and the Children. Their function may include providing quality of activities that involve the family in the usage of language Computation skills and Problem solving as well as Parental reinforcement of child's behaviour established in the school.

Educational institutions like Universities, NCERT, NIEPA, etc. can help in the development of resource materials suited to the needs of Resource centers.

In the present study it has been found that home environment does play a very vital role in the performance of the child at school and improvements are needed in low family environments. With this point of view the present study underlines that it is very important that society develops national policies and programmes to ensure that families are able to provide their children with an environment conducive to success in later life. Hence, policies can be worked out to provide the resources and nurturences that young children need to function as effective members of modern society.

Suggestion for Further Research

Generally one of the outcomes of conducting any research study is to generate avenues for further research. The present study entitled 'Impact of family environment on School performance of elementary school children, also points to the same directions, the related research workers may choose to opt for in the near future.

The results of the present study throw a valuable light on the usefulness of School –focussed parent child interactions on the school performance of elementary school children. But the present study is based on a sample drawn from a limited geographical area and is confined to class V students only. It would be appreciable if similar research efforts are put in with a sample drawn from wider geographical area and having a variety of subjects for further research studies.

Results of the present study indicate the importance of family environment on the school performance of elementary school children. However, taking into consideration the difference in parent – child interactions at different stages of development, similar studies may be conducted for Pre- school and secondary school students also.

Comparative studies covering different levels of education, i.e. pre-primary, primary, elementary, and secondary stages be also conducted to find out the impact of family environment on performance of student belonging to different age- groups.

Studies to develop resource material and design intervention strategies for the needy parents may also be carried out.

Evaluative studies may also be taken up to go into the effect of intervention strategies designed for the needy parents.

The present study was limited to similar school environment. Similar effort can be put in to conduct studies on different type of school

The present study was limited to similar school environment. Similar effort can be put in to conduct studies on different type of school environmental like Rural – Urban, Govt. – Private, Aided – Unaided.

Effect of school focussed interactions provided by different members in the family can also be studied.

Comprehensive studies of family environment characteristics covering Psycho – social characteristics as well as status characteristics, as associated with school performance of children may also be carried out.

Appendix-I
Construction of the Scale

Introduction

The construction of the scale was one of the important tasks in the present study. The study was family environment aimed at identifying environmental interactions within the family that influence the school performance of elementary school children. The investigator carried out a through study of the relevant literature. An overwhelming research evidence has focussed on the significance of home environment variables in the over all development of the child. Home environment has often been considered in terms of status characteristics such as income, education, and occupation of the parents etc. However research trends in the west advocate a move away from the rigidity of such status variables towards assessing what it is that parents actually do with their children like parent's interest in academic activities, knowledge of educational progress, quality of language used by parents, availability of guidance, opportunities for thinking and imagination etc. (Walberg ; Marjoribanks 1976). With this in view, five dimensions concerning school focused parent child interactions were identified to be included in the scale namely Achievement orientation; Cognitive stimulation; Recreational orientation; Home structure; and Language stimulation.

Achievement Orientation refers to extent of Parental concern reflecting their belief and attitude, for child's education and other activities, Knowledge of progress of the child and provision of facilities for achieving educational goal.

Cognitive Stimulation refers to encouragement and guidance to the child to indulge in thought provoking activities and opportunities made available to the child to develop thinking and imagination.

Recreational Orientation refers to extent and content of interaction during indoor and out door activities, (purpose of) use of mass media and use of books, library or other such facilities.

Home Structure dimension of family environment is confined to degree of importance given by family members to the value of clear organizations and work habits, extent to which set rules and procedures are used to run family life and degree of help and support family members provide to each other.

Language stimulation addresses itself to degree of importance shown to the quality of language used by parents / family members and opportunities made available to the child for expansion of vocabulary.

Pilot Survey

A pilot survey was conducted by visiting a number of schools and homes of students in order to get an insight into the type of school focussed parent child interactions within the family. It was decided to carry out informal interviews with parents, teachers, students and experts in the field. It was considered essential to ask them about the type of parent child interactions, which they felt, have a positive influence on a child's school performance. They were told that the interviewer wished to know what kind of interest parents took in their child's education and how they expressed it. The interviewer was particularly interested in knowing the points these people emphasized and were particular about. In other words, interviews were conducted to know what experts believed in general and what the parents do in particular. Initially 20 such interviews were conducted in the university campus area of Kurukshetra. The initial responses of teachers, students, parents and experts in the field, contacted during the pilot survey yielded significant information and an initial pool of items was obtained. Additional items were adapted from other existing tools.

The pilot survey thus enabled the researcher in discerning information from the actual field setting and helped in exploring the diverse facts of the problem for preparing the tools for study.

Family Environment Scale for Children

Information gathered during pilot survey revealed that a Child and a Parent may perceive the environment within the family differently. Therefore in order to know their responses individually, two forms of Family environment scales were developed one for the Children and the other for Parents.

Writing of Statements for Family Environment Scale (FES) for Children

On the basis of the study of literature, information gathered during the pilot survey and personal experiences, an exhaustive list of items pertaining to school focussed parent child interactions was prepared. While framing the statements for this purpose some suggestion given by Cannal and Kahn (1970) regarding preparation of such a tool e.g. frame of reference; level of information; social acceptance; form of statement; single item statement etc. were considered. The final list of items thus prepared was given to the language expert for vetting. The preliminary draft of the tool so constructed was given to some faculty members of Kurukshetra University for their expert comments. The same was modified in the light of their suggestions. This draft was given to the language expert for vetting and it was then considered fit for try-out.

Try-Out and Revision

The first draft of family environment scale thus prepared was given to a small group of students concerned, for the purpose of removing any ambiguities and to see if the items properly communicated what the same were intended to. This initial try-out lead to the further revision and refinement of the tool for its effectiveness.

After the initial try-out and the revision the first draft of the tool was administered to a larger group consisting of 47 students. In the light of their responses the necessary modifications were made and the first draft of the tool was prepared for the purpose of data collection. The first draft of Family environment scale consisted of 82 items. These belonged to five dimensions of Family environment viz. Achievement orientation; Cognitive stimulation; Recreational orientation; Home structure; and Language stimulation. Table 1 below provides dimension wise distribution of items on family environment scale for children.

Table 1

Distribution of Items on Various Dimensions of Family Environment Scale (FES) for Children

Sr. No.	*Dimensions of EFS*	*Number of Item*
1	Achievement orientation	(13)
2	Cognitive stimulation	(19)
3	Recreational orientation	(18)
4	Home structure	(19)
5	Language stimulation	(13)

Administration of the Scale For Item Analysis

After obtaining due permission from the concerned authorities the scale was administered to class v students in small groups of 30-35each, in the respective school premises by the investigator herself. Usual requirements for proper test administration like, quite, comfortable, welllit room, with ample space for each respondent to work,, were ensured. In order to establish good rapport, the investigator made introductory remarks appropriate to the situation. The help of class teacher was solicited in distributing the test booklets with a purpose to get cooperation from the subjects.

Sample

For the purpose of standardization of Family Environment Scale for Children the sample consisted of 370 students of class V.

Instructions

Purpose of the scale and instruction were printed on the title cover of each test booklet. However instructions were read aloud to the subjects while they followed them silently from the test booklets. It was made clear to the subjects that the statements included in the scale pertained to school focussed parent child interactions and they were requested to read each statement carefully. It was further emphasized that there was no right or wrong response to a statement and the answers entirely depended on one's own experiences and perceptions within the family. They were asked to tick mark any one of the three responses, which they feel is true or mostly true for them, in the box provided in front of the statement. Respondents were reminded to keep in mind that each statement had only one answer and they were told to feel free and respond according to how they felt. Simple clarification of word meanings, if any, was given on request but care was taken not to influence the direction of the respondent's responses. Further clarifications and difficulties, if any, were resolved and the subjects were asked to start giving the responses. When all the subjects in a particular group had completed the test, the investigator collected the test booklets. In the end she expressed her appreciation and thanks for their cooperation.

Scoring

Scoring procedure of FES is very simple and objective. Each item had three responses representing the kind of interaction in the family viz. a- indifferent, b- moderate, c- stimulating. Responses a, b, and c, were scored as 0, 1, and 2 respectively.

Direction of scores and their meaning

This scale measures school focussed parent child interactions. A high score indicates stimulating interactions reflecting Enriched family environment and a low score indicates Low family environment.

Item Analysis

A form of item analyses has been suggested by Edward (1957) as a basis for rejecting the statements in the method of summated ratings. The same method has been followed here. At first the data obtained for–370 children was arranged in ascending order. The top and bottom group of 92 each (25% as suggested by Edward) , then formed the criterion groups in terms of which to evaluate the individual statements. The discrimination power of each statement is then/was then calculated by testing the significance of mean difference between the two (high and low) criterion groups on a particular statement i.e. by calculating critical ratios (C.R.) for each statement.

This CR value is a measure of the extent to which a given statement differentiates between the high and low groups, in other words, the discrimination value. A CR value equal to or greater than 1.67 (using one tail test) is taken as an index of it's sufficient power of discrimination.(p-.05).In this way statement with a CR value equal to or greater than 1.67 of scale were selected and those falling below this value were rejected as non- discriminating statements.

In order to ensure a degree of homogeneity i.e. items on the scale must correlate significantly with the total scores, Item-Total score correlation for each dimension was computed.

Family environment scale for Parents

Similar procedure was followed for the construction of Family Environment scale for the parents. Intended meaning and contents of each of the 82 statement was kept the same, however the statements were worded as per the need. For the purpose of standardization of Family Environment Scale for Parents, the sample consisted of 175 parents of students of class V.

On applying the two criterion, i.e. item discrimination and item- total score correlation, it was found that discrimination value of five items in the child form and six items in the parent form did not fulfil the criterion. On the basis of correlation, it was found that value of four items in the child form and three items in the parent form was below .1485.

Therefore considering these two aspects item that did not fulfil any of the criteria in either of the forms was dropped. Thus twelve items were not considered for the final form of family environment scale (FES) for children and parents. Test-retest reliability and split half reliability of the final tool was computed and after following proper procedure for its construction the final form of the tool consisted of 70 items. Accordingly a subject could score minimum of '0' and maximum of '140'.

Table 2

Distribution of Items on Various Dimensions of Final form of Family Environment Scale (Fes) for Children and Parents

Sr.No.	*Dimension of FES*	*No. of items*
1	Achievement orientation	(10)
2	Cognitive stimulation	(16)
3	Recreational orientation	(15)
4	Home structure	(16)
5	Language stimulation	(13)

Reliability of Family environment scale for children

After four weeks time interval the scale was re-administered to 55 students. On comparing the response sheets three cases of reckless attempt were detected and therefore not considered for scoring. The test retest reliability coefficient indicating the stability of measurement over a period of time came out to be 0.943. Split –half reliability of the FES for Parents was calculated. Reliability coefficient of the half test was 0.848 and by using Spearman-Brown prophecy formula, the reliability coefficient of the whole test came out to be 0.918.

The reliability coefficients indicate a high degree of stability in the measurement made by this scale.

Reliability of Family environment scale for parents

After four weeks time interval the scale was re-administered to 55 parents. On comparing the response sheets five cases of reckless attempt were detected and therefore not considered for scoring. The test retest reliability coefficient indicating the stability of measurement over a period of time came out to be 0.902. Split –half reliability of the FES for Parents was calculated. Reliability coefficient of the half test was 0.828 and by using Spearman-Brown prophecy formula, the reliability coefficient of the whole test came out to be 0.906.

Validity of Family Environment Scales for Children and Parents

In order to establish the content validity of family environment scale for children and parents the face validity criteria was applied. The preliminary draft consisting of about 100 items was given to the experts judges and they were asked to give their opinion on whether

(i) items were related to the particular dimensions of the scale

(ii) the item measured what they were purported to measure.

On the basis of the experts opinion the items that were not relevant to particular dimension were rejected. In this way the content validity of the family environment scales has been established.

The procedure used for item analysis satisfies the internal consistancy criteria of validity.

Purpose of family environment scale was to measure family environment in terms of school – focussed parent child interactions. The investigator could not locate a scale, similar in nature to one that was developed for the present study. Therefore, the method of criterion related validity was not applied.

Bibliography

Addington, D.G. (1977). "Effects of Parental Involvement of Mathematics Achievement at Eight, Tenth and Twelfth Graders". *Dissertation Abstracts International*, Vol. 57, No. 10.

Anderson, E.L. (1994). "The Effect of Parental Involvement on Academic Achievement", *Dissertation Abstract International*, 55, (2).

Basavayya,D. (1974). *Effect of Billingualism on Language Achievement.* CIIL Mysore: 1974.

Belsky, J. (1990). 'Parental and Non-parental Child Care and Children' Socio-emotional Development. A Decade in Review'. *Journal of Marriage and Family* 52(4), 885-903.

Bevli, U. (1990). Researches in Child Development: A Book of Readings, NCERT, New Delhi.

Bhatnagar, J.K. and Sharma, M. (1992). "A study of Relationship between Parental Education and Academic Achievement in a semi-rural Setting", *Psychological Studies*, 37(2 &3), pp.126-129.

Bing, Elizabeth. (1963). "Effect of Child Rearing Practices on Development of Differential Cognitive Abilities" *Child Development*, 34, 3, 631-649.

Bloom,B.S. (1964). *Stability and Change in Human Characteristics"* In Early Childhood Education – Rediscovered Readings, Joe. L, Frost, Holt, Rinehart & Winston, Inc. New York (pp. 241-265).

Bloom,B.S. (1981). *All Our Children Learning.* New York: McGraw-Hill.

Bradley, Caldwell and Elardo (1977) "Home Environment, Social Status and Mental Test Performance" *Journal of Educational Psychology*, 1977, Vol. 69 (6), 697-701.

Buch, M.B. (ed.) (1974). A Survey of Research in Education, Baroda: Centre of Advanced Study in Education, M.S. University.

Buch, M.B. (ed.) (1979). Second Survey of Research in Education, (1970-78). Baroda: Society for Educational Research and Development.

Buch, M.B. (ed.) (1991). Fourth Survey of Research in Education, (1978-1983), New Delhi: N.C.E.R.T.

Buch, M.B. (ed.) (1991). Fourth Survey of Research in Education, (1983-1988), New Delhi: N.C.E.R.T.

Cannel,C.F., and Kahn, R.L., (1970). *Collection of Data by Interviewing.* In: L. Festinger, and D. Katz (Eds.), Research Methods in Behavioural Sciences. New Delhi: Amerind Publishing Co.

Chatterjee, S., Mukherjee, M. & Banerjee, S.N. (1972), "Effect of Certain Socio-economic Factors on the Scholastic Achievement of the School Children". *Indian Journal of Psychology*, 47, 133-151.

Chen, C., & Uttal, D.H. (1988), "Cultural Values, Parents' beliefs, and Children's Achievement in United States & China". *Human Development*, 31, 351-358.

Cherian, V.I. (1992). "The Relationship between Parental Aspiration and Academic Achievement of Xhosa Children from Monogamous and Polygynous Families". *Journal of Social Psychology*, 132, 271-273.

Chilampikunnel, M.A. (1995). "Parental Involvement and Students Performance and Selfesteem in Sub-urban and City Parochial Elementary (K-6) Schools". *Dissertation Abstracts International*, Vol. 56, (5).

Clinton, I. Chase (1974). '*Measurement for Educational Evaluation*', Addition-Wesley Publishing Company Inc. Philippines.

Coleman, J.S. et al. (1966). *"Equality of Educational Opportunity"* Office of Education, US Department of Health, Education and Welfare, Washington, D.C.

Crimm, J.A. 1993. "Parental involvement and academic achievement: A meta-analysis". *Dissertation Abstracts International*, Vol. 53, (7).

Dave, R.H., (1963). "The Identification and Measurement of Environmental Process Variables Related to Educational Achievement", Unpublished Doctoral Dissertation, University of Chicago.

Ebel, Robert, L., (1965). '*Measuring Educational Achievement*', Prentice Hall, New Jersey.

Edwards, A.L. (1957). "*Techniques of Attitude Scale Construction*". Appleton Century Crafts, Inc.

Epstein, J.L. (1983a). "*Effects on Parents of Teachers Practices of Parent Involvement*". Baltimore, M.D. Centre for Social Organization of Schools, Johns Hopkins University (Report No. 346).

Epstein, J.L. (1983b), "Longitudinal Effects of Family-School-Person Interactions on Student Outcomes", *Research in Sociology of Education and Socialization*, 4, 101-127.

Fehramann, P.G., Keith,T.Z., & Reimers, T.M. (1987). "Home Influence of School Learning: Direct and Indirect Effects of Parental involvement on High School Grades".*Journal of Educational Research*, Vol. 80(6), 330-337.

Fogelman, K.R. and Goldstein H., (1976). "Social Factors associated with changes in educational attainment between 7 and 11 years of age", *Educational Studies* 2(2): 95-100.

Fraser, E. (1959). "Home Environment and the School", University of London Press, London.

Garrett, H.E. (1971), "*Statistics in Psychology and Education*", Vakils, Feffer and Simsons Pvt. Ltd., Bombay.

Goodnow, J., Collins W.A. (ed) (1990). '*Development According to Parents: The Nature, Sources and Consequences of Parents'* Ideas Erlbam Hove.

Griswold, P.A. 1986, "Family Outing Activities and Achievement Among fourth Graders in Compensatory Education Funded Schools", *Journal of Educational Research*, Vol. 79, (5), 261-266.

Grolnick, W.S. & Slowiaczek, M.L. (1994). "Parents' involvement in Chidlren's Schooling: A multidimensional conceptualization and motivational model", *Child Development*, Vol. 63, 237-52.

Grover,S. (1979). "Parental Aspiration as Related to Personality on School Achievement of Children", Ph.D. Psychology, Pan.Univ. In: *Fourth Survey of Research in Education*, NCERT, pp. 823.

Havighurst R.J. and Levine D.V. (1979). "*Socialization and Education*", University of Missouri; Kansas City, Allyn and Bacon Inc. Toronto.

Henderson, R.W., Bergan, J.R. & Hurt, M. (1972), "Development and Validation of the Henderson Environmental Learning Process Scale". *Journal of Social Psychology*, 88, 185-196.

Hess, R.D. and Halloway S.D. (1984). *"Family and School as Educational Institutions:* In Parke R.D. (eds.) Review of Child Development Research: Vol. 7. The Family University of Chicago Press.

Hess, R.D., Holloway, S.D., Dickson, W.P., & Price, G.G. (1984), "Maternal Variables as Predictors of Children's School Readiness and later Achievement in Vocabulary and Mathematics in Sixth Grade", *Child Development*, 55, 1902-1912.

Homchaudhri, S. "An Analytical Study of Correlates of Academic Performance of College Students (Tribal) of Mizoram", *Third Survey of Research in Education*, 1978-83,NCERT, pp. 667.

Jagannadhan, K. (1985). "The Effects of Certain Socio-psychological Factors on the Academic Achievement of Children Studying in Classes V to VII "Ph.D. SVU. In *Fourth Survey of Research in Education*, NCERT, pp. 826.

Keeves, J.P. (1972), *'Educational Environment and Students'* Acheivement', Almquist and Wiskell, Stockholm.

Kellaghan T and Macnamara J. (1972). "Family Correlates of Verbal Reasoning Ability". *Developmental Psychology*, 1972, (7) 1, 49-53.

Kellaghon J., Shoan Anesay B, Blown B.S. (1993). *'Home Environment and School Learning*', Jessey-Bass, San Francisco-California.

Khare, S. (1997). "Home Learning Environment and Creative Writing Ability of Elementary School Children". *Journal of Educational Research and Extension*, 33(3), 126-131.

Krishnan, P.A. (1977). "Non Intellectual Factors and their Influence on Academic Achievement", *Psychological Studies*, (22) 23-29.

Lall, R. (1984). "Child Rearing Attitudes, Personal Problems and Personality Factors as Correlates of Academic Achievement". Ph.D. Psychology, Bhagalpur University. In: *Fourth Survey of Research in Education*, NCERT, p. 833.

Laosa, L. M., Sigel, I.E. (1982). "*Families as Learning Environment for Children*", Plenum Press – New York, London.

Lin, C.A., Atkin, D.J. (1989). "Parental Mediation and Rulemaking for Adolescent Use of Television and VCRs". *Journal of Broadcasting and Electronic Media*, 33, pp. 53-67.

Maitra, K. (1985). "Affective Correlates of the Gifted Underachievers", Ph.D. Edu. Del. Univ. In: *Fourth Survey of Research in Education*, NCERT, p. 834.

Malini, I. Muralidharan, R., Bevli, U. "A Study of Children between the Ages of 5½ to 11 – Effects of Environmental Process Variables on School Achievement and Cognitives Development". Report of the Core Study of Delhi Centre, NCERT (1978).

Marjoribank, K. (1972). "Ethnic and Environmental Influences on Mental Abilities". *The American Journal of Sociology*, 78, 323-337(a).

Marjoribanks K. (1979). *Families and Their Learning Environment. An Empirical Analysis* : Routledge and Kegan Paul. London.

Marjoribanks, K. (1972). 'Environmental, Social Class and Mental Abilities', *Journal of Educational Psychology*, 63(2), 103-109.

Marjoribanks, K. (1979). "Families and their Learning Environments: An Empirical Analysis". Routledg and Kegan Paul, London.

McCartney K, Howley, E. (1992). *Parents as Instruments of Intervention in Home Based Pre-school Programs*. In Okagak, L. Steinberg R.J. (eds.) (1992) Directors of Development: Influences on the Development of Children's Thinking Erlbaum Hillsdale, New Jersey.

Mertens, Donna M. (1998). *'Research Methods in Education and Psychology: Integrating Diversity with Qualitative and Quantitative Approaches'*. Sage Publication, Thousand Oaks London. New Delhi.

Miller, S. (1988). "Parents' Beliefs about their Children: Cognitive Development", *Child Development* 59(2): 259-85.

Misra, G. & Tiwari, B.K. (1990). "Environment an Cognitive Development", In: Bevli (ed.) Researches in Child Development: A Book of Readings NCERT, 1990.

Misra, G. (1978). "An Experimental Study of Cognitive Process as a Function of Prolonged Deprivation", Unpublished Ph.D. thesis Gorakhpur University. In: Bevli, U.K. (Eds) Research in Child Development – A Book of Reading (1990).

Misra, G. (1983). "Deprivation and Development: A Review of

Indian Studies", *Indian Educational Review*, 18, 17-32.

Misra, G., & Shukla, A. (1979). "Experimental Deprivations and Development of Serial Memory", *Psychologia,* 22, 155-163.

Misra, G. & Shukla, A. 1984. "Recognition of Pictorial Material as a function of Deprivation and Age" *International Journal of Behavioural Development*, 95-103.

Moline, D.R. (1999). "The Parental Involvement Student Achievement". *Dissertation Abstract International*. Vol. 39 (1).

Moos, R.G. & Moos, B.S. (1981). "*Family Environment Scale Manual*", Palo Alto, CA: Consulting Psychologists Press.

Muller, C. (1993). "Parental Involvement and Academic Achievement: An Analysis of Family Resources Available to the Child". In B. Schneider & J.S. Coleman (Eds.), Parents, their children and School (pp. 77-113). Boulder, Co: Westview.

Muralidharn, R., "A Study of the Effect of Environmental Process Variables on Children, Achievement in Primary School", In: Bevli, U. (Ed.) Research in Child Development: A Book of Readings, NCERT, 1990.

Murdock, G.P. (1949). *'Social Structure'*, In: The Sociology of Education; An Introduction, Morrish Ivory 1978, 2nd Ed.. George Allon & Unwin Ltd., London.

Murphy, G., and Likert, R., (1937). *'Public Opinion and the Individual'*, New York; Harper.

Musgrove, F. 1966. "*Family, Education and Society*, Routledge, Kegan Paul – London.

Paul, S. (1986). "A Study of Cognitive Styles of High School Students of Home Science in Relation to Age, Achievement, Home Environment and Social Class"; Ph.D., Edu. Agra Univ. In: *Fourth Survey of Research in Education*, NCERT, p. 843.

Peaker, G.F., 1967. *The regression analysis of the national survey.* In: The International Encyclopaedia of Education 2nd Ed. Vol. 4.

Popham, J.W. (1988). "*Educational Evaluation*", Prentice Hall, New Jersey, p. 167-168.

Rao, N. (1978). 'A Study of the Social-Psychological Correlates of Social Development of High School Children in Grades VIII, IX and X in some High School of Bangalore City', Unpublished Ph.D. thesis

(Edu.) Ban. U. 1978.

Rao, S.N. (1977), *"Concept Development in Children"*, Tirupati: S.V. University.

Rayan, Adams, Gulloth, Wessberg & Hampton (1995). "The Family-School Connection-Theory, Research and Practice", Sage Publication, New Delhi.

Saini, B.K. (1977). "Academic Achievement as a Function of Economic Status and Educational Standard of Parents". *Psychological Studies*, 22, 34-45..

Salunke, R.B. (1979). "A Study of Home Environment, SES and Economic management in relation to the academic achievement of the I Year College Student of M.S. University, Baroda", *Third Survey of Research in Education 1978-83*, NCERT pp. 685.

Sarkar U. (1983). "Contribution of Some Home Factors on Children's Scholastic Achievement", Ph.D. Psychology. Cal. University. In: *Fourth Survey of Research in Education*, NCERT, p. 849.

Scott-Jones, D. (1984), "Family Influence on Cognitive Development and School Achievement", *Review of Research in Education*, 11, 259-304.

Segine, R. (1983). *"Parents' Educational Expectations and Children's Academic Achievements: A Literature Review"*, Merrill-Palmer Quarterly, 29, 1-23.

Sinha, D. 1977. "Some Social Disadvantage and Development of Certain Perceptual Skills". *Indian Journal of Psychology*, 52, 115-132.

Stevenson D.L., Baker D.L. (1987). 'The Family-school Relation and the Child's School Performance'. *Child Development*. 58(5), 1348-57.

Stevenson, D.L., Baker D.P. (1987). "The Family School Relation and the Child's School Performance" *Child Development*, 58, 1348-1357.

Swift; D.F. (1967). "Family Environment and 11+ Success: Some Basic Preconditions". *British Journal of Educational Psychology*, 37, 10-12.

Thakur, L. (2001). "Effect of Home Environment on Intelligence and Educational aspiration". *Journal of Education and Psychology*,

59(4) 8-15.

Trivedi, V. (1987). "A Study of the Relationship of Parental Attitude, Socio-economic Background and Feeling of Security among the Intermediate Students and their Academic Achievement", Ph.D., Edu. Luck. Univ. In: *Fourth Survey of Research in Education*, NCERT, pp. 843.

Trusty, J. (1998). Family influences on educational expectations of late adolescents". *The Journal of Educational Research*, Vol. 91(5), 260-270.

Tynell Burgess – *'Home and School'* England: Penguin Books Ltd.

Visser, D. (1987). "The Relationship of Parental Attitude and Expectations to Children's, Mathematics Achievement Behaviour", *Journal of Early Adolescence*, 7, 1-12.

Walberg, H.J. and Marjoribanks K. (1973), "Differential Mental Abilities and Home Environment: A Canonical Analysis", *Developmental Psychology* 1973, Vol. 9.3, 363-368.

Wentzel, K.R., Feldman,S.S., & Weinberger, D.A. (1991) "Parent Child Rearing and Academic Achievement in boys: The Meditational Role of Socio-emotional Adjustment". *Journal of Early Adolescence*, 11,321-339.

Whang, P.A. & Hancock, G.R. (1994). "Motivation and Mathematics Achievement: Comparison between Asian-American and Non-Asian Students. *Contemporary Educational Psychology, 19*, 302-322.

White, K.R. (1982). "The Relationship between Socio-economic Status and Academic Achievement", *Psychological Bulletin*, 91(3); 461-481.

Wolf R.M., 1964, 'The Identification and Measurement of Environmental Process Variables Related to Intelligence', Unpublished doctoral dissertation, University of Chicago.

Wood, J., Chapin, K., & Hannah, M.E. (1988), "Family Environment and its Relationship to Underachievement", *Adolescence*, 23, 283-290.

Yusof,A. (1984). "The Relationship between Family Communication Self Concept and Academic Achievement of Adolescent in Some Schools of Pelating Malaysia". *Dissertation*

Abstract International, Vol. 46(4).

Zhao, Y.M. (1997). "Social Class and Differences in Parental Expectation and Involvement in Education: A Study of Two Schools in Urban Shangai". *Dissertation Abstracts International*. Vol. 35, No.1.

Index

A

Achievement Orientation, 21, 147
Addington's Study, 36
Anderson's study, 35
Asian-American and non-Asian
  students maths achievement, 36

B

Beliefs and attitudes of parents, 20
Bhatnagar and Sharma study, 35

C

Chen and Uttal's Study, 33
Cherian's Study, 35
Child, 17, 135
  development of, 17
  influence of family on, 18
Child Rearing Practice (Bing Study), 27
Chilampi Kinnel's Study, 36
Chinese and US Mothers
  comparison, 33
Coefficient of Correlation of School
  Performance
  and family environment, 52
  and elementary school children, 53
  and socio-economic status, 53
Cognitive Stimulations 20, 22, 147
Comparison of
  Ratios of School performance, 66,
    77, 102, 109
  Mean School performance, 66
  T Ratios of School performance
  different
    as perceived by Children, 76,
      83, 101
    as perceived by parents, 109,
      122
Confinements/limitations of Study, 139
Crimm study, 35
Cultural Background impact on school
  performance, 20

D

Deprivation and development studies,
  31
Development status of the child, 23
Different Mental ability and home
  environment, 29
Difference in Mean School performance
  scores (perceived by parents
  of overall family environment, 67
  on achievement orientation, 69
  on cognitive stimulation, 71
  on recreational orientation, 72
  on home structure, 74
  on language simulation, 75
Difference in Mean school performance
  scores at different levels of family
  environment (perceived by
  children) of children belonging to

High intelligence groups, 79, 86-90, 104
Moderate intelligence groups, 80, 91, 105
low intelligence groups, 82, 95, 107
Similar intelligence, 84

E

Elementary education, 23
Emotional background impact on school performance, 20
Environment definition, 19
Epstein Study, 31
Expectation of maths achievement by parents, 33

F

Family
context, 22, 136
term, 18
outing and achievement, 33
Family environment
and school performance 32, 130
meaning, 24, 138
Family Environment Scales (FES), 42 147-48
for children (writing of), 42
first draft, 43, 149
try out, revision, 149
final form, 44
for parents, 44, 151
administration, 149
standardization, 150
scores/meaning, 150
item analysis (Edward), 151
Reliability, 152
validity, 152
Family Environment
impact on similar interest groups, 131
children perception, 50, 130
parents perception, 130
Findings of Study, 129

G

Griswold Study, 35
Grolnick and Sloniaczeks study, 35

H

Hess et al stduy, 32
Home-environment factors and performance (Studies), 29, 31
Homa Chandhuri's Study, 31
Home Structure, 22, 148
Home environment, 19
and creative writing ability, 36
and intelligence, 37
Home based intervention programmes, 20
Hypothesis of differential growth rate, 139
(Blooms study), 28

I

Index of educational environment (Dave study), 28
Intelligence and School performance, 130
Intervention programme for parents/ Children, 132-33, 143

J

Jagannathan Study, 32

K

Kellaghan and Macnamarsa Study, 29
Keeves Study on family contex, 29
Khare's Study, 36

L

Lall Study, 32
Language stimulation, 22, 148

Learning attitude and academic achievement, 32
Learning environment of the home study, 29
Literature review importance of, 27

M

Maitra Study, 32
Mean School Performance Scores (as percieved by children), 56
- overall family environment, 56
- achievement orientation, 57
- cognitive stimulation, 59
- recreational orientation, 61
- home structure, 63
- language stimulation, 64

Mean School Reformance scores comparison
- as perceived by children, 77, 102
- as perceived by parents, 109, 123

Mean School performance Difference at different levels of family environment (as perceived by children) of Children belonging to
- High intelligence groops, 79, 86-90, 104
- moderate intelligence groups, 80, 93, 105
- low intelligence groups, 82, 95, 105
- similar intelligence, 84

Mean School performance Difference at different levels of family environment (as perceived by parents) of children belonging to
- high intelligence groups, 111
- low intelligence groups, 118
- moderate intelligence groups, 114

Methodology of investigation, 39
Misra Study, 31
Mothers educational level, 53
Motivation and mathematics archievement, 36
Murdock on family, 18

N

Non Verbal Test of Intelligence, 44

O

Out of home experience, 20

P

Parent teacher organization, 20
Parental influence on intelligence test performance, 28
Parental
- aspirations, 35
- attitude studies, 33

Parental imolvement in education, 35-36
- in social activities, 33

Parental expectation and education level, 37
Parent-teacher organization, 20
Parental education level study, 29-30, 35
Paul study, 33
Peaker study on home environment factors, 28
Pilot survey of Schools , 42, 148
Procedure for data collection, 46

R

Reading with children (Study on), 32
Recreational Orientation, 22
Results interpretation and analysis, 49
Research Studies on School performance
- justification 22-23, 135

objectives, 24, 136
method, 140
sample, 140

S

Sampling, 40
Sarkar's study, 31
School environment, 17-18
School performance, 22, 24, 137
and parents perception, 51
coefficient of correlation, 51
in relation to intelligence, 52
differentials in elementary school, 55
as perceived by children, 55
phenomenon of, 49
Seginer Study, 31
Selection for study of schools/respondents, 41
Socio-economic status
and school performance, 20, 130
inventory, 45
Societal Changes, 22
Socio-psychological characteristics of family impact on school performance, 21, 25, 32
Statistical Techniques used in data analysis, 47, 140
Stevenson and Baker Study, 33

T

Thakur Study, 37
Tools Used for Study, 41, 140
T Ratios Comparison obtained for School performance differentials of similar intelligence groups
as perceived by children, 76, 83, 101
as perceived by parents, 109, 122
Try-out and Revision of FES, 149
Trivedi Study, 33
Trusty study, 37

V

Verbal Reasoning ability study of, 29
Vissar study, 33

W

Walbeg and Marjon banks study, 29
Whang and Hancock, 36

Y

Yusof Study, 32